Dr. Onyója Momoh is an international family law expert specializing with in-depth knowledge of the work of the HCCH children's conventions. She was called to the Bar in 2010 (*Gray's Inn*) and practices exclusively in family law. Shortlisted for *Rising Star – Barrister/Advocate of the Year* at the Women in Law Awards 2020, she has been consistently recognized as a leading junior in children law by the Legal 500 UK since 2017. Onyója undertook her LLM, Ph.D., and EU-funded post-doctoral research all in the area of international child abduction, and also specializes in cases involving international child protection and intercountry adoption. She appears at all levels of the Family Court and the Court of Appeal and receives instructions to provide expert advice in proceedings in the UK and abroad.

Alongside her practice, she lectures private international law (family law) at the University of Aberdeen, serves on affiliated non-profit boards, and is widely published in the area. She also delivers training, lectures, and presentations globally. In recent years, Onyója has been involved in high-level advisory and advocacy work with Government ministries (particularly in Nigeria and sub-Saharan Africa), the judiciary, and charities. She has also been invited as an expert to present at forums such as the Hague Conference on Private International Law, the European Commission, and the UK House of Lords Justice and Home Affairs Committee.

# A Practical Guide to the 1996 Hague Child Protection Convention in Public Law Children Proceedings

# A Practical Guide to the 1996 Hague Child Protection Convention in Public Law Children Proceedings

Onyója Momoh Ph.D.

Law Brief Publishing

Published 2025 by Law Brief Publishing, an imprint of Law Brief Publishing Ltd
30 The Parks
Minehead
Somerset
TA24 8BT

www.lawbriefpublishing.com

Paperback: 978-1-916698-88-8

*For S and V*

# PREFACE

Since the United Kingdom's departure from the European Union, the 1996 Hague Convention on Jurisdiction, Applicable Law, Recognition, Enforcement, and Co-operation in respect of Parental Responsibility and Measures for the Protection of Children has taken on a more prominent role in the landscape of child protection and care proceedings. The treaty, now often spoken in practice, yet not always fully understood in its operational aspects, remains a fixture in legal discourse—frequently invoked like a wishing well: acknowledged, rehearsed, and sent on its way, with the hope that its mechanisms will quietly and effectively deliver the desired outcome. The Convention provides a vital framework for international cooperation in safeguarding children, particularly in matters of child welfare across borders. This book explores how the Convention has gained significant traction in practice, particularly in the context of intercountry cooperation on child protection cases, and the increasing reliance placed upon it by UK authorities and other contracting States. Key issues are explored, including addressing the specific powers granted by the Convention regarding jurisdiction, applicable law, the recognition and enforcement of foreign orders. By highlighting practical and procedural matters in applying the 1996 Hague Convention, the book will provide insight into the evolving landscape while examining the day-to-day realities of implementing cross-border child protection measures and offering recommendations that strengthen its utility.

The manuscript was completed on 28 February 2025, and I have aimed to state the law as reflected in the sources available to me at that date.

*Onyója Momoh*
*March 2025*

# CONTENTS

# CHAPTER ONE

# INTRODUCTION

The 1996 Hague Convention on Jurisdiction, Applicable Law, Recognition, Enforcement, and Co-operation in respect of Parental Responsibility and Measures for the Protection of Children[1] has long been an underused powerhouse in cases where children's lives span multiple borders. The 1996 Hague Convention was born out of necessity. By the late 20th century, the limitations of existing legal frameworks became apparent. For instance, the 1980 Hague Convention on the Civil Aspects of International Child Abduction provided a remedy for wrongful removals and retentions, yet it did not address the broader complexities of international child welfare and protection. Cross-border care proceedings, the placement of children abroad, and jurisdictional conflicts called for a more comprehensive instrument. The 1996 Hague Convention filled this gap, offering a cohesive legal structure for international child protection. Nevertheless, its widely recognised counterpart, the 1980 Hague Convention has likely led to the 1996 Convention being viewed more as an ancillary tool, operating in quieter legal corridors rather than the authoritative legal framework it was designed to be. This book aims to reframe that perception, highlighting the 1996 Convention as an essential component of international child protection law. With cross-border public law cases increased— in 2021, nearly 29% of children were born to non-UK women, the Convention's utility has become more evident than ever.

1 To be referred to as "the 1996 Hague Convention", "the 1996 Convention". Also known as the 1996 Hague Child Protection Convention.

As such, the 1996 Hague Convention has quietly evolved into a vital tool for international child protection, especially in cross-border care proceedings. The Convention was designed to establish a clear framework for jurisdiction, applicable law, recognition, and enforcement in international child protection. At its core lies the principle that a child's habitual residence should govern jurisdiction, ensuring stability and continuity in legal decision-making. It also introduces mechanisms for cooperation between contracting States, facilitating the transfer of jurisdiction where necessary and ensuring the enforcement of protective measures across borders.

For legal practitioners working within the realm of international child protection, the focus is not merely on interpreting legal texts but on navigating the complexities of practical application. This includes determining fundamental jurisdictional issues such as where the child is habitually resident, which court has jurisdiction, whether bilateral or multilateral treaties apply, and how protective measures can be enforced across borders. The 1996 Hague Convention provides clarity in these areas, particularly in public law cases where the State's protective role is central. Unlike private law disputes, where parental autonomy plays a central role, public law cases engage the protective machinery of the State. The Convention acknowledges this distinction, providing mechanisms for international cooperation when a child's welfare necessitates intervention. Articles 8 and 9, for instance, allow for the transfer of jurisdiction when another State is better placed to make determinations in a child's best interests. Article 33 introduces mandatory consultation when a child is to be placed abroad, ensuring that the receiving State is adequately prepared for the child's arrival. Recognition and enforcement provisions under Articles 23 and 24 are equally crucial. The effectiveness of any legal order depends not only on its issuance but on its ability to be implemented across jurisdictions. The Convention seeks to prevent legal limbo, ensuring that decisions made in one State are respected in another.

Further, the Convention aligns with broader international principles, including those enshrined in the United Nations Convention on the Rights of the Child (UNCRC), affirming that children should have a say in matters affecting them. Whether through the appointment of a guardian ad litem or judicial mechanisms that take the child's views into account, legal practitioners must ensure that the child's voice is not lost amid procedural complexities. Finally, of course the application of the Convention is not without challenges. Differences in national laws, procedural obstacles, and issues of non-recognition can complicate enforcement, requiring careful navigation by practitioners.

This book aims to provide a practical roadmap for legal professionals dealing with the 1996 Hague Convention, blending theoretical foundations with actionable insights. It includes case law, procedural guidance, and references to official documentation from the Hague Conference on Private International Law ("HCCH"), offering a foundational understanding of the Convention's operation in public law children cases.

# CHAPTER TWO

# THE 1996 HAGUE CONVENTION

The 1996 Hague Convention provides a structure for effective reciprocity and international co-operation in child protection matters.[2] The Convention provides jurisdiction to issue protective measures based on the child's presence in the refuge State, allowing courts handling return applications to implement necessary safeguards. The 1996 Hague Convention deals with a wide range of issues, including parental disputes over custody or contact, the protection of runaway teenagers, refugee and internationally displaced children, placement of children abroad in foster or institutional care, and specific powers of representation. It is this framework that also influences the appropriate steps in placing or receiving a child from abroad. As such, practitioners are conversant with the difficulties that arise in the absence of reciprocal common framework for international cooperation.

---

2 Permanent Bureau of the HCCH, 'Approach Global Event: the 25th Anniversary of the HCCH Child Protection Convention' (The Hague, 2021) <https://assets.hcch.net/docs/0edc5a90-9a94-402e-8fb4-3b9d27a6aab5.pdf>

## 2.1 Background to the 1996 Hague Convention

The principles of the "protection of minors"[3] and "childhood in danger"[4] were central to of the creation of the 1996 Hague Convention, enhancing the legal protection of children in international custody disputes but also in abduction cases. Shortly after it came into force in 2002, the UK ratified the Convention in 2003[5] as part of its EU membership at the time . This allowed the treaty to be incorporated into domestic law, without the need for separate primary legislation.[6] However it was nearly a decade later – on 1st November 2012 – that the 1996 Hague Convention officially came into force in the UK. Following the repeal of the European Communities Act 1972 as part of the UK's departure from the EU, the legal status of the 1996 Hague Convention was reinforced through the enactment of the Private International Law (Implementation of Agreements) Act 2020. By doing so, the UK preserved its commitment to the Convention and secured its effectiveness as a key international instrument for the protection of children. With the legal

---

3 Permanent Bureau of the HCCH, 'Explanatory Report: Convention of 19 October 1996 on Jurisdiction, Applicable Law, Recognition, Enforcement and Co-operation in Respect of Parental Responsibility and Measures for the Protection of Children' (*Proceedings of the Eighteenth Session (1996), Tome II, Protection of children*) by Lagarde, referred to as 'Explanatory Report' or 'Lagarde Report', para 1.

4 Explanatory Report, para 3.

5 HCCH 1996 Hague Convention 'Status Table', available at <https://www.hcch.net/en/instruments/conventions/status-table/?cid=70>

6 Facilitated under the framework of the European Communities Act 1972, this meant that the United Kingdom could adopt EU law and international agreements without the need for further primary legislation.

framework established through the 2020 Act, the 1996 Hague Convention has become the primary international instrument[7] governing child protection in the UK. The application of the 1996 Hague Convention has led to several notable case law developments, demonstrating how courts interpret and apply the Convention's provisions. In addition to fostering international cooperation, the 1996 Hague Convention provides a framework for the UK to establish best practices in handling cross-border child protection cases. Whereas the number of contracting States (57)[8] remains a limitation in its wide-reaching applicability, interactions with Convention countries demonstrate the practical benefits of the instrument in resolving complex international child protection issues. As more countries adopt the Convention, the collective strength of international co-operation will grow, providing a more unified and enhanced protection of children globally.

The Convention is supported by several key documents that aid in its interpretation and practical application including the Explanatory Report authored by Professor Paul Lagarde, the Practical Handbook on the Operation of the 1996 Child Protection Convention and the

7 Replacing "Brussels *IIbis*"*: Council* Regulation (EC) No 2201/2003 of 27 November 2003 concerning jurisdiction and the recognition and enforcement of judgments in matrimonial matters and the matters of parental responsibility, repealing Regulation (EC) No 1347/2000 [2003] OJ L338/1; superseded by the "Recast Regulation" or "Brussels II*ter*". Council Regulation (EU) 2019/1111 of 25 June 2019 on jurisdiction, the recognition, and enforcement of decisions in matrimonial matters and the matters of parental responsibility, and on international child abduction ST/8214/2019/INIT OJ L 178, 2.7.2019.

8 As of 28 February 2025.

Implementation Checklist.[9] The HCCH regularly convenes Special Commission meetings to assess and enhance the practical operation of the Convention[10] as well as to ensure that the Convention remains responsive to evolving global dynamics[11] while strengthening the legal safeguards for children. These gatherings serve as platforms for Contracting Parties to discuss challenges, share best practices, and propose improvements in cross-border child protection measures, the latest being the Eighth Meeting of the Special Commission, held from 10 to 17 October 2023.[12]

## 2.2 Objectives of the Convention

Fundamentally, the 1996 Hague Convention is grounded in the principles of international cooperation and the best interests of the child. By encouraging States to work together and recognize each other's protective measures, it promotes legal certainty and stability for children in international situations. At its core, the Convention seeks to enhance the protection of children by establishing clear rules on jurisdiction, applicable law, and the recognition and enforcement of protective measures. Through its carefully structured legal

---

9 See also Permanent Bureau of the HCCH, *Practitioners' Tool: Cross-Border Recognition and Enforcement of Agreements Reached in the Course of Family Matters Involving Children* (The Hague, 2022).

10 The review of its practical operation is considered alongside the 1980 Hague Convention.

11 In example: Permanent Bureau of the HCCH, *The Application of the 1996 Child Protection Convention to Unaccompanied And Separated Children*, The Hague, 2024.

12 Permanent Bureau of the HCCH, Preliminary Documents and Conclusions available at <https://www.hcch.net/en/publications-and-studies/details4/?pid=8488&dtid=57>

mechanisms, the Convention seeks to safeguard every child regardless of their circumstances or the jurisdictions involved. It is divided into seven chapters: Scope of the Convention; Jurisdiction; Applicable Law; Recognition and Enforcement; Co-operation; General Provisions; Final Clauses. The preamble to the 1996 Hague Convention makes clear that: -

> "Considering the need to improve the protection of children in international situations,
>
> Wishing to avoid conflicts between their legal systems in respect of jurisdiction, applicable law, recognition and enforcement of measures for the protection of children,
>
> Recalling the importance of international co-operation for the protection of children,
>
> Confirming that the best interests of the child are to be a primary consideration..."

The objectives of the 1996 Hague Convention are clearly articulated at the outset. As per Article 1:

The objects of the present Convention are -

a) to determine the State whose authorities have jurisdiction to take measures directed to the protection of the person or property of the child;

b) to determine which law is to be applied by such authorities in exercising their jurisdiction;

c) to determine the law applicable to parental responsibility;

d) to provide for the recognition and enforcement of such measures of protection in all Contracting States;

e) to establish such co-operation between the authorities of the Contracting States as may be necessary in order to achieve the purposes of this Convention.

Of note, and as with any private international law instrument, the Convention aims to prevent conflicts of law between legal systems, ensuring that different national laws do not create legal uncertainty or obstruct a child's right to stability and care. By doing so, a Convention objective is to foster cooperation between States, ensuring that the best interests of the child remain a primary consideration in all decisions affecting them. Another of the Convention's key objectives is to support children caught in international parental disputes over custody, access, or contact by determining the law to be applied and the appropriate measures of protection. As these cases often arise when parents live in different countries or when one parent seeks to or relocates abroad with a child, the Convention's mechanisms aims to resolve these disputes efficiently.

With the protection of children being a key objective, the 1996 Convention also extends to children who are internationally abducted and where protective measures are sought[13] as well as the protection of unaccompanied minors, and of children placed abroad in alternative care arrangements, particularly when these arrangements do not fall under the 1993 Hague Convention on Protection of Children and Co-operation in Respect of Intercountry Adoption. This includes cases where children are placed in foster care, *kafala*, or

13 Momoh.O, '*The need for cross-border protective measures in return proceedings*' in Trimmings K, Dutta A, Honorati C and Zupan M (eds), Domestic Violence and Parental Child Abduction (1st edn, Intersentia 2022)

other institutional settings in another country. By ensuring that such placements are properly regulated and recognized across jurisdictions, the Convention helps prevent exploitation, neglect, or trafficking of vulnerable children. Children who are victims of cross-border trafficking, exploitation, and sexual abuse also fall within the Convention's protective scope.[14] Thus, while the 1996 Hague Convention addresses a wide range of international child protection issues, this book will concentrate on its application in public law care proceedings. Furthermore, although this book focuses on the Convention's application in public law cases, the case law discussed will inevitably extend beyond this scope where relevant.

## 2.3 Measures Available Under Article 3 of the 1996 Hague Convention

Article 3 encompasses a broad range of legal provisions relating to parental responsibility, custody, access, guardianship, child placement, supervision of care, and the management of a child's property. Article 3 of the Convention provides that: –

The measures referred to in Article 1 may deal in particular with -

a) the attribution, exercise, termination or restriction of parental responsibility, as well as its delegation;

b) rights of custody, including rights relating to the care of the person of the child and, in particular, the right to

---

[14] Permanent Bureau of the HCCH, *'Practical Handbook on the operation of the Hague Convention of 19 October 1996 on Jurisdiction, Applicable Law, recognition, Enforcement and Co-operation in respect of Parental responsibility and Measures of the Protection of Child'* (2014) para 63 (hereafter '1996 Convention Practical Handbook') para 1.2-1.3.

determine the child's place of residence, as well as rights of access including the right to take a child for a limited period of time to a place other than the child's habitual residence;

c) guardianship, curatorship and analogous institutions;

d) the designation and functions of any person or body having charge of the child's person or property, representing or assisting the child;

e) the placement of the child in a foster family or in institutional care, or the provision of care by kafala or an analogous institution;

f) the supervision by a public authority of the care of a child by any person having charge of the child;

g) the administration, conservation or disposal of the child's property.

The measures listed in Article 3 are not exhaustive but are provided as examples seeking to present a broad scope, while acknowledging that such measures vary across legal system.[15] For example, from an English perspective, while "Special Guardianship" is a well-established legal status, it remains unfamiliar in many other jurisdictions, particularly in EU civil law systems. However, the broad scope of Article 3 helps support the position as to the distinction between parental responsibility held by a parent and that of a special guardian. In public law cases where the final care plan is a special guardianship order in favour of e.g. a relative, the fact that that special guardian has the final say or overarching parental responsibility would, in certain cases, be

15 Explanatory report, para 18-20.

seen as a protective measure. Article 3 allows scope for practitioners to comfortably explore the measures of protection envisaged in spite of, amongst others, linguistic particularities.[16]

Parental responsibility, as covered under Article 3(a), warrants an autonomous interpretation. It can arise through various mechanisms under domestic law. In some jurisdictions, parental responsibility is automatically granted, such as when a child is born to married parents. In others, it may require specific actions, such as recognition by an unmarried father, the subsequent marriage of parents, or a formal agreement.[17] Additionally, courts or administrative authorities may assign parental responsibility. The term "attribution" in the Convention is designed to encompass all aforementioned approaches, ensuring its broad applicability. Indeed, under English law, parental responsibility is acquired through several different mechanisms, all of which fall within the broad scope of Article 3(a) of the 1996 Hague Convention. Married parents automatically share parental responsibility upon the birth of their child. For unmarried fathers, parental responsibility can be obtained by being named on the birth certificate (if registered after 1 December 2003), through a formal parental responsibility agreement with the mother, or by securing a court order. Additionally, stepparents and second female parents in same-sex relationships can acquire parental responsibility through

---

16 Explanatory Report, para 20 where Lagarde observes that "Certain English-speaking delegations, in particular that of the United Kingdom, pointed out that the terms 'custody' and 'access' were replaced in their legislation by different expressions: 'residence order' for 'custody', 'contact' or yet 'visitation' for 'access'. The Convention cannot claim to employ expressions which suit the linguistic particularities of all the States represented. What counts is the meaning which the Contracting States have wanted to give to the words employed".

17 1996 Convention Practical Handbook, para 3.20.

agreement or court order. Local authorities may also be granted parental responsibility in cases where a child is subject to a care order.

Article 3(b) covers rights of custody and access,[18] aligning its definitions with the 1980 Hague Child Abduction Convention[19] to maintain consistency between the two treaties. Rights of custody include determining where a child resides and who has the authority to make decisions about their care. Rights of access, which encompass in-person visits as well as remote communication, ensure meaningful contact with a non-custodial parent or other relatives. The Convention also envisages guardianship and similar institutions under Article 3(c) as measures of protection, as well as the appointment and responsibilities of those entrusted with a child's care under Article 3(d). Placement in foster care, institutional settings, or alternative care arrangements like kafala is addressed in Article 3(e). Additionally, Article 3(f) mandates public authority supervision in cases where a child is under the care of another person. Lastly, Article 3(g) provides safeguards for the administration, conservation, and disposal of a child's property, ensuring financial protection and responsible management.[20]

---

18 Ibid, para 3.2; 4.22 (see “situation A”)

19 Article 5(b), 1980 Hague Convention.

20 Ibid, para 13.71.

# CHAPTER THREE

# JURISDICTION

Articles 5 to 14 of the 1996 Hague Convention focuses on jurisdictional issues. The jurisdiction to make decisions about a child's welfare is primarily determined by the child's habitual residence, as stipulated in Article 5. Article 5 ensures that the court of the child's habitual residence has jurisdiction over issues of parental responsibility and protection. Article 6 provides that the authorities of a contracting State where refugee or internationally displaced children are present, or where a child's habitual residence cannot be established, have jurisdiction as outlined in Article 5. In general terms, Articles 7 to 10 address situations where jurisdiction is shared or where different States may have concurrent jurisdiction, emphasizing the need for coordination between States to avoid conflicts. Article 11 provides that in urgent cases, the authorities of any contracting State where a child or their property is present have jurisdiction to take necessary protective measures, with such measures lapsing once the appropriate authorities under Articles 5 to 10 take action or once measures from another State are recognized.

## 3.1 Articles 5 and 6: Habitual Residence

The concept of habitual residence is fundamental to the operation of the 1996 Hague Convention, ensuring that jurisdiction lies with the State most closely connected to the child, and UK case law has played a significant role in shaping the interpretation of this principle. However, before exploring case law, it is noteworthy that the Explanatory Report provides insight into how habitual residence should be understood, influencing both international and domestic applications of the Convention. Lagarde's Report refers to the contracting Sate of the habitual residence of the child as the State having "principal jurisdiction"[21] but also refers to the possibility of a change of residence. The Eight Meeting of the Special Commission[22] reiterated that the change of habitual residence is a question of fact for the competent authority seised to be conducted "diligently and without delay",[23] although such authority may consult with other States for further information. As such, there are aspects of the Convention that has required interpretation within case law. For example, Article 5 does not specify a particular date for determining a child's habitual residence in the context of measures to be taken, or when jurisdiction "passes"[24] to another contracting State; neither does the Explanatory Report or 1996 Convention Practical Handbook[25] provide guidance on its interpretation. From an English perspective however, case law[26] has established that the relevant date is the date the court is seised.

---

21 Explanatory Report, pg. 553

22 Permanent Bureau of the HCCH, *Eighth Meeting of the Special Commission on the Practical Operation of the 1980 Child Abduction Convention and the 1996 Child Protection Convention*, Conclusions and Recommendations, (The Hague, 2023), referred to as 'SC Eight Meeting, Conclusions and Recommendations' para 62.

23 SC Eight Meeting, Conclusions and Recommendations, para 62.

24 Explanatory Report, para 38.

25 See 1996 Convention Practical Handbook generally.

26 *See Re London Borough of Hackney v P and Others* [2023] EWCA Civ 1213; *Derbyshire CC v Mother* [2022] EWHC 3405 (Fam) and H v R [2022] EWHC 1073 (Fam).

Historically, the UK courts approach to determining habitual residence crystalised in 2013, when the UK Supreme Court[27] preferred the Court of Justice of the European Union's test ('CJEU') for habitual residence.[28] According to the CJEU:

> "To ensure that the best interests of the child are given the utmost consideration, the Court has previously ruled that the concept of 'habitual residence' under Article 8(1) of the Regulation corresponds to the place which reflects some degree of integration by the child in a social and family environment. That place must be established by the national court, taking account of all the circumstances of fact specific to each individual case (see A, paragraph 44)".[29]

This ruling shifted the focus towards the child's experience, emphasizing that habitual residence is determined by actual connections to a particular country rather than parental intentions. Further, the Supreme Court also confirmed that this interpretation applies uniformly to both the 1996 Hague Convention and Brussels II Revised (as it then was), ensuring consistency across legal frameworks. The Lagarde Explanatory Report offers additional insight

---

27 In example: *In the matter of A (Children) (AP)* [2013] UKSC 60 (*A v A and Another (Children: Habitual Residence) (Reunite International Child Abduction Centre intervening)* [2014] AC 1), *In re C and another (Children) (International Centre for Family Law, Policy and Practice intervening)* [2019] AC 1, *In re R (Children) (Reunite International Child Abduction Centre and others intervening)* [2015] UKSC 35, [2016] AC 76. See also *Re B (A Child: Custody Rights, Habitual Residence)* [2016] 4 WLR 156.

28 See (Case C-497/10 PPU) [2012] Fam 22, [2011] 1 FLR 1293. *Cf* previous decision in *Proceedings brought by A* (Case C-523/07) [2010] Fam 42, [2009] 2 FLR 1: "some degree of integration" [44]

29 *Mercredi v Chaffe*, para 47.

into how habitual residence should be approached, underlining two key observations that remain highly relevant. (i) a child's habitual residence remains unchanged if they temporarily leave[30] their country for reasons such as vacation, school attendance, or access visits. This ensures that short-term absences do not disrupt jurisdictional continuity, preventing unnecessary legal dispute. (ii) a change in habitual residence results in both the loss of the previous habitual residence and the acquisition of a new one. While this transition often involves a lapse of time, the acquisition of a new habitual residence can also be instantaneous—for instance, when a family relocates to another country. As such, as a question of fact to be assessed by judicial authorities, a child's habitual residence is not automatically tied to their primary caregiver's residence or the child's nationality.[31]

In exploring habitual residence, practitioners are encouraged to consider the evidential value of the following factors when presenting their client's case: the child's physical presence, school or nursery enrolment, registration at GP or other medical services, and other matters supporting their connection to the country. For a more detailed perspective, practitioners may observe the comprehensive guidance at paragraphs 17 and 18 of *In re B (A Child) (Custody Rights: Habitual Residence)* [2016] EWHC 2174 (Fam), [2016] 4 WLR 156. Notably as summarised in the decision *in re B*, the so called "modern concept" of habitual residence adopts guidance from *A v A*, an overall formulation subsequently endorsed by the majority of the UK Supreme Court in *In re C and Another (Children) (International Centre for Family Law, Policy and Practice intervening)* [2019] AC 1 [56].

30 Explanatory Report, para 40.

31 See in example discussion in *R v B (Stranded: Habitual Residence: Forum Conveniens)* [2020] EWHC 1041 (Fam).

## 3.2 Article 7: The Consequence of a Wrongful Removal or Retention

The intersection of parental child abduction, parental responsibility, and child protection is often complex and overlapping. As regards to public law matters, local authorities may be involved from the outset as holders of parental responsibility seeking the child's return or may become engaged in proceedings with a history of abduction. Article 7 of the 1996 Hague Convention establishes a "special"[32] jurisdictional rule in cases of wrongful removal or retention of a child. It ensures that the authorities of the child's habitual residence before the abduction "keep their jurisdiction"[33] until specific conditions are met. These include the child acquiring habitual residence in another State and either "each person, institution or other body having rights of custody has acquiesced"[34] in the removal or retention, or the child has lived in the new State for at least one year, no return request is pending, and the child is "settled in his or her new environment."[35] A removal or retention is considered wrongful when it breaches custody rights under the law of the child's habitual residence and when those rights were being exercised or would have been but for the removal. Custody rights may arise "by operation of law,"[36] a court or administrative decision, or a legally binding agreement. While the initial jurisdiction remains, authorities in the new State may only take "such urgent measures under Article 11 as are necessary for the protection" of the child's person or property. This ensures wrongful

---

32 See 1996 Convention Practical Handbook, para 13.3.

33 Article 7(1)

34 Article 7(1)(a)

35 Article 7(1)(b)

36 Article 7(2)

removals do not automatically shift jurisdiction while balancing the child's need for stability.

### 3.3 Article 8 and 9: The Transfer of Jurisdiction

For mutual 1996 Hague contracting States, the legal framework vis-á-vis the transfer of jurisdiction can be found under Articles 8 and 9.[37] The procedure for transferring proceedings (incoming and outgoing) under Articles 8 or 9 of the 1996 Hague Convention is outlined in Family Procedure Rules 2010 (rules 12.61-12.67). This process ensures that cases involving children are transferred between States to place legal responsibility with the most appropriate authority. Articles 8 and 9 allow courts to transfer jurisdiction if another State is better positioned to assess the child's best interests, ensuring decisions align with the child's welfare across international borders. An application for the transfer of jurisdiction under Articles 8 or 9 of the 1996 Convention can be made using Form C68,[38] typically by a party to the proceedings. While such applications are often informal, they can also be submitted through the respective Central Authorities or directly to the court. Outgoing requests refer to transfers from

---

37 See case law: *Re M (Children) (1996 Hague Convention: Request to Exercise Jurisdiction)* [2016] EWHC 2535 (Fam); *Re D (Care Proceedings: 1996 Hague Convention: Article 9 Request)* [2021] EWHC 1970 (Fam); *Warrington Borough Council v T and Others* [2021] EWFC 68, [2022] Fam 107; *AM and GM v KL and VL* [2023] EWFC 15, *Haringey LBC v N* [2024] EWFC 151 and *Child and Family Agency (Ireland) v Mother* [2021] EWHC 1774 (Fam), *Child and Family Agency (Ireland) v Mother* [2021] EWHC 1774 (Fam)

38 https://www.gov.uk/government/publications/form-c68-application-for-international-transfer-of-jurisdiction-to-or-from-england-and-wales

England and Wales, while incoming requests involve transfers to England and Wales.

Article 8 allows a court with general jurisdiction (typically where the child is habitually resident) to request another contracting State to assume jurisdiction if that State is better placed to assess the child's welfare. Amongst other matters, this ensures that child protection decisions are made where they can be most effectively enforced. Whereas Article 9 permits a court in a contracting State that does not have general jurisdiction to request authorization to assume jurisdiction if it considers itself better placed to assess the child's best interests. Essentially, enabling authorities in a country other than typically the child's country of habitual residence to request that the home country relinquish jurisdiction so they can take necessary protective measures. This is particularly relevant where children from other jurisdictions are placed within this legal system and how international safeguards are applied to protect their welfare. Thus, Articles 8 and 9 of the Convention establish a flexible system for determining which country's authorities should handle child protection cases when it is in the best interests of the child. These provisions function as a reversible mechanism for *forum non conveniens* and *forum conveniens*,[39] ensuring that jurisdiction is exercised by the most appropriate State. In terms of facilitating the transfer of jurisdiction, communication between competent authorities is encouraged.[40] As recently reaffirmed at the HCCH Eighth Meeting of the Special Commission, it was noted that jurisdictional issues under Chapter II[41] of the 1996 Hague Convention form a "complete and closed system." While this framework prevents conflicting

39 Explanatory Report, para 52.

40 See also President's Guidance, Public law children cases with an international element, pg. 2.

41 Chapter II – Jurisdiction: Articles 5-14

jurisdictional claims among Contracting Parties, it may also present challenges. Therefore, effective communication between competent authorities is encouraged when assuming, taking, or transferring jurisdiction under the Convention.

The cases *Child Family Agency (Ireland) v Mother* [2021] EWHC 1774 (Fam) and *Haringey LBC v N* [2024] EWFC 151 provide insights into the application of Articles 8 and 9. *Child and Family Agency (Ireland) v Mother* was the first application made by the CFA under Article 8 of the 1996 Hague Convention for a transfer request (as opposed to Article 15 of the Brussels II Revised Regulation (*as it then was)).* The case involved AB, an infant born in Ireland to a British mother, who was placed under the emergency care of the Child and Family Agency of Ireland (CFA) shortly after birth. After the child's birth in Ireland, the Child and Family Agency initiated care proceedings and subsequently sought to transfer jurisdiction to the courts in England and Wales under Article 8 of the 1996 Hague Convention. The Irish court granted this request, recognizing the child's substantial connection with the UK due to the family's history and prior involvement with social services including the fact that AB's siblings were residing in the UK under supervision orders. Upon the case's transfer, the High Court in England and Wales accepted jurisdiction, noting that the criteria under Article 8 were satisfied: the child had a significant connection to England and Wales, and that the authorities were better placed to assess the child's best interests, given their extensive knowledge of the family's background. Much can also be observed about the value of collaboration between the authorities including though the judicial network. Of note, the court adopted authorities that applied Article 15 of Brussels II Revised, the court accepted that there was no material difference[42] between the Regulation and the provisions under the 1996 Hague Convention. As

42 *Child and Family Agency (Ireland) v Mother*, para 18.

such, the procedures set out in previous decisions were adopted,[43] with the court in *the matter of HJ (A Child)* [2013] endorsing the comprehensive guidance given by Cobb J (*as he then was)* at paragraphs [9] [10] [22]-[40], at [35-40]:

> 35. It is clear from Article 15(5) that the request for transfer must be considered judicially rather than administratively. Hence this hearing. However, a question arises whether the function of a court in the requested State determining a 'transfer request' is limited to a consideration of "best interests" only, or whether the court has a wider remit to review for itself all of the criteria for transfer. In considering this question, I must be careful not to arrogate to myself a function properly within the exclusive jurisdiction of the foreign court: see Munby J (as he then was) in AB v JLB (Brussels II Revised) [2009] 1 FLR 517.
>
> 36. My reading of Article 15(1) and Article 15(5), taken together, leads me to the conclusion that my function is limited to a "best interests" determination only. Article 15(1) appears to contemplate that it is in the courts of the Member State having jurisdiction as to the substance of the matter, requesting transfer, that the question of whether the child has a "particular connection" with the court of another Member State which would be "better placed to hear the case" should be considered. The role of the court of the requested State appears, by Article 15(5), to be limited to a consideration of "best interests" having regard to "the specific circumstances of the case"; the "best interests" evaluation will necessarily not be as profound as on a full hearing of an application for substantive relief with the benefit of the full evidence. While

43 *Re LM* [2013] EWHC 646 (Fam) and *In the matter of HJ (A Child)* [2013] EWHC 1867 (Fam*)*

> not relevant for my determination on these facts, if a court of a requested State considered that, contrary to the determination of the requesting State, the child did not in fact have a "particular connection" with the requested State in accordance with Article 15(3), and/or that the court of the request-ed State was not in fact "better placed to hear the case", it would surely reasonably easily reach the conclusion that it was not in the "best interests" of the child to accept the request for transfer, and would therefore decline it.
>
> 37. This approach appears to be consistent with the text of the Practice Guide to BIR which, al-though only advisory, is nonetheless of assistance. [...]
>
> 38. Having regard to all of the circumstances of this case and drawing upon the factors identified in paragraph 34 above in particular, I am wholly satisfied that it is in the best interests of LM that the public law proceedings should indeed be transferred to this jurisdiction. It follows that the courts of England and Wales will accept the request for transfer of the proceedings, and jurisdiction to determine the case concerning LM.
>
> 40. The Article 15 transfer takes effect between the general jurisdiction of the requesting State and the general jurisdiction of the requested State. I need therefore to turn next to the arrangements domestically for giving effect to the transfer."

In contrast, *Haringey LBC v N* considered an outgoing transfer request following the mother's unilateral removal of the child, T, to Poland during ongoing care proceedings in England. At that time, only an Interim Supervision Order was in place, which did not grant the local authority parental responsibility. The court determined that by being seised of the care proceedings, it held rights of custody over T. Consequently, T's removal to Poland was deemed wrongful under Article 7 of the 1996 Hague Convention. The court considered whether to acquiesce to T's removal, which would shift jurisdiction to Poland under Article 7(1)(a). However, it concluded that Article 7 is not a transfer provision but rather determines whether jurisdiction has shifted due to wrongful removal. The court emphasized that the appropriate mechanism for transferring jurisdiction is Article 8, which allows a court with general jurisdiction to request another contracting State to assume jurisdiction if that State is better placed to assess the child's best interests. Applying Article 8, the court found that the Polish authorities were better positioned to evaluate T's welfare, given his habitual residence there, and thus transferred jurisdiction accordingly. At paragraph 57, Macdonald J observed that:

> "For the reasons set out above, T has acquired habitual residence in another State for the purposes of Art 7(1). Pursuant to Art 7(2), for the removal of T by his mother to have been wrongful for the purposes of Art 7(1) it must have been in of breach of rights of custody attributed to a person, an institution or any other body under English law and those rights must have been being actually exercised or would have been so exercised but for the wrongful removal. In circumstances where the removal of T was in breach of the father's rights of custody, but he has acquiesced to that removal, the first question is whether rights of custody for T are attributed to the court for the purposes of Art 7(2) of the 1996 Hague Convention by virtue of the court being seised of proceedings under Part IV of the Children Act 1989? I am satisfied that they are."

In both cases, the courts carefully evaluated the child's connections to the respective jurisdictions, the location of evidence, and which authorities were better positioned to make informed decisions regarding the child's welfare. These decisions appear to be consistent with the Convention's emphasis on flexibility and international cooperation to protect children's best interests in cross-border situations.

Of comparative relevance is the High Court decision in *B v N (No. 2) (Art 7 and Transfer of Jurisdiction)* [2024] EWHC 17 (Fam). In this case, a child was wrongfully removed from the UK to Germany by the father. The English High Court examined whether it retained jurisdiction under Article 7, which maintains existing jurisdiction based on the child's habitual residence at the time of wrongful removal. The court clarified that Article 7 does not establish a new jurisdictional basis but preserves the original jurisdiction under Article 5. Consequently, Article 8 remains applicable, allowing for the transfer of jurisdiction to another State better positioned to assess the child's best interests. In this case, considering the child's strong connections to Germany and expressed desire to remain there, the English court requested the German court to assume jurisdiction, emphasizing the importance of international cooperation and the child's welfare in cross-border disputes. This ruling reinforces that wrongful removal does not automatically alter jurisdiction and that any retention of jurisdiction must prioritize the child's best interests, ensuring proper international cooperation in child protection matters. Indeed, in *B v N (No.2) (Art 7 and Transfer of Jurisdiction))*, the court ruled differently from Arbuthnot J's decision in *A (A Child) (Abduction: Jurisdiction: 1996 Hague Convention)* [2021] EWHC 581 (Fam) by deciding that Article 8 still applied even when jurisdiction is kept under Article 7 of the 1996 Hague Convention.

### 3.4 Article 11: Urgent Measures of Protection

Article 11 of the 1996 Hague Convention provides that:

1. In all cases of urgency, the authorities of any Contracting State in whose territory the child or property belonging to the child is present have jurisdiction to take any necessary measures of protection.

2. The measures taken under the preceding paragraph with regard to a child habitually resident in a Contracting State shall lapse as soon as the authorities which have jurisdiction under Article 5 to 10 have taken the measures required by the situation

3. The measures taken under paragraph 1 with regard to a child who is habitually resident in a non-Contracting State shall lapse in each Contracting State as soon as measures required by the situation and taken by the authorities of another State are recognised in the Contracting State in question.

As noted, Article 11 enables the court in "all cases of urgency" to take "necessary measures" of protection on the premise that the child is present in that jurisdiction at the time such measures are taken. In addition, it is expected that the provisions under Article 11 enables measures taken to be recognised in all the contracting States.[44] Firstly, it is for the competent authority seised of the matter and in which the child or their property is present to determine whether the circumstances warrant the qualifying term "urgent." There is no definition of urgency[45] although given that it is a derogation from the

44 Explanatory Report, para 72.

45 ibid para 68.

general rules of jurisdiction,[46] urgency should be interpreted strictly.[47] However, in the 1980 Hague Child Abduction Convention proceedings in *Re J (A Child)*[48] Baroness Hale considered that an abduction case should warrant the exercise of Article 11.[49] Lagarde observes that "urgency" under Article 11 arises when the usual remedial actions under Articles 5 to 10 of the 1996 Hague Convention are insufficient[50] and may result in "irreparable harm"[51] to the child. Lagarde further notes that the Commission deliberately decided to "abstain from setting out what measures might be taken on the basis of urgency",[52] this intentional flexibility allows courts to adapt their responses to the specific risks involved in each case. In public law children cases, the threshold of significant risk of harm is almost always comparable to a harm that is irreparable. Indeed, Article 7(3) defers to Article 11 to address the issue of urgent measures to protect the child or property of the child.[53] Ultimately, it is for judicial authorities to use their discretion in each case to determine whether

---

46 1996 Convention Practical Handbook, para 6.3.

47 ibid.

48 *Re J (A Child) (Reunite International Abduction Centre and others intervening)* [2015] UKSC; [2015] 3 WLR 1827. See also Edward Devereux, '*Re J*: the 1996 Hague Convention in the Supreme Court' (2016) International Family Law, 21-24.

49 ibid [39].

50 Explanatory Report, para 68.

51 ibid.

52 Explanatory Report, para 70. However, the lack of definition holds the potential risk of inconsistent practice. See also See Nigel Lowe, 'The Impact of the 1996 Convention on International Child Abduction', Division 5, Chapter 5, Clarke Hall & Morrison on Children (2017) 888.

53 Article 7(3) 1996 Hague Convention.

the case is "urgent".[54] In practice, *Re J (A Child)* observed that the assessment of necessity and urgency requires a holistic approach.[55]

Further, Article 11 underscores that any measures taken must be "necessary" for the protection of the child or their property. Notably, the drafters of the 1996 Convention intentionally refrained from defining "necessity."[56] The Practical Handbook on the 1996 Convention advises that it is ultimately for judicial authorities to determine what measures are "necessary" in response to an urgent situation. Accordingly, the interpretation of "necessary" should be considered alongside "measures of protection." As aptly observed by Munby J in H-*L (A Child) (Care Proceedings: Expert Evidence)* [2013] EWCA Civ 655, [2013] 2 FLR 1434: 'The short answer is that 'necessary' means necessary. It is, after all, an ordinary English word…This court said it "has a meaning lying somewhere between 'indispensable' on the one hand and 'useful', 'reasonable' or 'desirable' on the other hand", having the "connotation of the imperative, what is demanded rather than what is merely optional or reasonable or desirable."'[57] In *B v B*,[58] Mostyn J determined that protective measures—including non-molestation and contact restrictions—could be made under Article 11 and recognized under Article 23 across contracting States, supporting the return of a child to Lithuania. In this case, it was found that the safeguards eliminated the grave risk of

---

54 ibid.

55 *Re J (A Child)* [33] (Baroness Hale).

56 Practical Handbook on the 1996 Hague Convention, para 6.7.

57 *H-L (A Child) (Care Proceedings: Expert Evidence)* [2013] EWCA Civ 655, [2013] 2 FLR 1434 [3]- [4]. See also discussion in E. Devereux, '*Re J*: the 1996 Hague Convention in the Supreme Court' (2016) International Family Law.

58 *B v B* [2014] EWHC 1804 (Fam).

harm that would otherwise justify refusing return on the basis of Article 13(1)(b).

## 3.5 Article 13: Conflicts of Concurrent Jurisdictions in Courts & *lis pendens*

Article 13 of the 1996 Hague Convention provides that:

> 1) The authorities of a Contracting State which have jurisdiction under Articles 5 to 10 to take measures for the protection of the person or property of the child must abstain from exercising this jurisdiction if, at the time of the commencement of the proceedings, corresponding measures have been requested from the authorities of another Contracting State having jurisdiction under Articles 5 to 10 at the time of the request and are still under consideration.
>
> 2) The provisions of the preceding paragraph shall not apply if the authorities before whom the request for measures was initially introduced have declined jurisdiction.

Concurrent proceedings have become increasingly common, raising "positive"[59] conflicts of jurisdiction. Often engaging the *lis pendens* rule, this principle dictates that when proceedings involving the same parties and the same subject matter are pending in different jurisdictions, the court first seised (i.e., the court where proceedings were first initiated) typically has priority in deciding the matter. This principle is particularly relevant in international children cases where multiple jurisdictions may be involved. Note however that the

59 Where more than one State has jurisdiction as opposed to "negative" conflict of jurisdiction where no State has jurisdiction.

principle of *lis pendens* under Article 13 does not apply in urgent cases where measures of protection is sought (Article 11) or provisional measures (Article 12), which take precedence regardless of jurisdictional conflicts.[60] As such, Article 13 addresses situations where the authorities of multiple contracting States may have jurisdiction over a child protection matter. It outlines how potential conflicts of jurisdiction should be resolved, aiming to prevent overlapping actions. Specifically, Article 13 requires that if authorities in one contracting State are already considering measures to protect a child's person or property, the authorities in another contracting State, with jurisdiction over the same child, must refrain from taking similar measures if those measures are under consideration elsewhere.

The term "corresponding measures"[61] is not explicitly defined in the Convention. However, it can be inferred that the term refers to requests that are similar in substance[62] across both contracting States.[63] For example, if one contracting State is dealing with a child's custody case while another State is addressing protective measures related to the child's property, the latter may proceed with its case if the matters are not equivalent. In other words, a court in one jurisdiction may be seized with divorce proceedings which automatically addresses related child maintenance matters, whereas in another jurisdiction, the court focuses exclusively on child arrangements. This suggests that "corresponding measures" must be fundamentally related for Article 13 to apply. Another issue is the challenge for the authorities of a "second seised" State in determining whether corresponding measures have been requested from the first contracting State and whether those measures are still under consideration. If for example, the English

---

60 1996 Convention Practical Handbook, paras 6.8,6.9 and 7.4.

61 Article 13(1) 1996 Hague Convention.

62 1996 Convention Practical Handbook, para 4.31.

63 Explanatory Report, para 79.

court are the second jurisdiction seised, and there is clear evidence that the first State is already handling the case, the English court should abstain from exercising jurisdiction. However, in some cases, the parties involved may not be forthcoming with sufficient evidence regarding the status of the case in the first contracting State. In such situations, the English court may need to directly contact the relevant authorities in the first contracting State to clarify whether proceedings are still ongoing and if they qualify as corresponding measures. This ensures that both jurisdictions are aligned in their efforts to protect the child.

Article 13 continues to be applicable as long as the initial proceedings in the first contracting State are ongoing. However, it does not apply if the first contracting State declines jurisdiction. According to the Explanatory Report,[64] this means that the authorities of the contracting State that first takes jurisdiction can relinquish their authority to the English court if it is deemed more suitable. This renunciation of jurisdiction is similar to the transfer provisions outlined in Articles 8 and 9 but with key differences. Transfer under Article 8(1) will bring to end jurisdictional conflict under Article 13.[65] Specifically, the second contracting State already has jurisdiction over the matter, and the decision to relinquish jurisdiction can be made unilaterally. Despite this, to ensure the child's protection, good practice dictates that the two contracting States communicate with each other to avoid gaps in protection, ensuring that no conflicting decisions are made that could jeopardize the child's well-being.

In *B v N (No. 2) [2024]*, *lis pendens* was raised where the key question was whether the English court should retain jurisdiction under Article 7, given the child's wrongful removal, or whether the German courts,

---

64 ibid, para 80.

65 ibid

where later proceedings had begun, should take over. The English court ultimately ruled that while Article 7 preserves jurisdiction based on habitual residence at the time of removal, it does not override Article 8, which allows for the transfer of jurisdiction if another country is better placed. The court observed that: -

> "...jurisdiction is transferred to the German court pursuant to Art 8(1), the current lis subsisting by virtue of Art 13(1) as a result of the prior proceedings under Part II of the Children Act 1989 will come to an end. In the circumstances, I am not satisfied that Art 13 of the 1996 Convention constitutes a reason in this case for concluding that the German court is not better placed to assess X's best interests." [66]

Since the child had significant ties to Germany and had expressed a wish to remain there, the court decided to cede jurisdiction to Germany, reinforcing that *lis pendens* alone does not dictate the outcome—the child's best interests remain the overriding factor.

In summary, Article 13 aims to prevent jurisdictional conflicts between contracting States, ensuring that multiple States do not take conflicting measures concerning the same child's protection. By promoting communication and cooperation, fostered by practitioners (and in some instances judicial network) through the appropriate platform, the Convention seeks to prioritize the child's safety and welfare, while balancing the need for legal clarity and efficient handling of protection measures across borders.

---

[66] Ibid, para 69

# CHAPTER FOUR

# APPLICABLE LAW

Articles 15 to 22 of the 1996 Hague Convention establish rules on applicable law. They cover the law applicable to protective measures,[67] parental responsibility without judicial or administrative intervention,[68] third-party protection,[69] and other general provisions.[70] Article 15 provides that:

> (1) In exercising their jurisdiction under the provisions of Chapter II, the authorities of the Contracting States shall apply their own law.
>
> (2) However, in so far as the protection of the person or the property of the child requires, they may exceptionally apply or take into consideration the law of another State with which the situation has a substantial connection.
>
> (3) If the child's habitual residence changes to another Contracting State, the law of that other State governs, from the time of the change, the conditions of application of the measures taken in the State of the former habitual residence.

---

[67] Article 15, 1996 Hague Convention

[68] Article 16-18, 1996 Hague Convention

[69] Article 19, 1996 Hague Convention

[70] Article 20-22, 1996 Hague Convention

As a rule of thumb, the primary principle is that pursuant to Article 15, authorities exercising jurisdiction under the Convention apply their own law, the *lex fori*. This principle ensures consistency and predictability in legal proceedings in, e.g. England and Wales, so that the English courts would apply domestic law (such as the 1989 Children Act) when making decisions. However, the English Courts may, in exceptional circumstances consider the use of the law of another State if the child's situation has a substantial connection to it, e.g., *lex causae*. If a child's habitual residence changes, the law of the new residence applies to any existing protective measures. Article 16 states that parental responsibility arises, or ceases based on the law of the child's habitual residence, whether by operation of law, agreement, or unilateral act. If the child moves, existing parental responsibility remains unless the new State's law grants responsibility to someone else. The exercise of parental responsibility follows the law of the child's habitual residence,[71] and it may be modified or terminated under the Convention's measures.[72] Article 19 protects third parties who transact with a child's representative based on the law of the State where the transaction occurs. If the representative had apparent authority under domestic law, the transaction remains valid unless the third party knew the law of another State governed parental responsibility. Articles 20 and 21 clarify that these rules apply even if they designate a non-contracting State's law. However, Article 22 allows refusal if such application would be "manifestly contrary"[73] to public policy, taking into account the child's best interests.

71 Article 17

72 Article 18

73 Article 22.

# CHAPTER FIVE

# RECOGNITION AND ENFORCEMENT

## 5.1 Article 23(1): Recognition

Article 23 (1) of the 1996 Hague Convention sets out the foundational rule on recognition whereby:

> 'The measures taken by the authorities of a Contracting State shall be recognised by operation of law in all other Contracting States'.

The term recognition "by operation of law" means that the measures can be recognised in the requested State and have effect without the need to instigate any further proceedings in that State.[74] The measure to be recognised can be evidenced by way of written documentation or in urgent cases, by telephone.[75] Further, using a certificate pursuant to Article 40 would also facilitate the process of recognizing measures automatically under Article 23(1). In some ways, Articles 23 and 26 go hand in hand. Once the enforceable measure is taken in one contracting State, Article 26 provides that the measure can be recognized and enforced in another country, provided that an interested party formally requests it. Thereafter, Article 28 provides that once the measure has been declared enforceable or registered for enforcement, it has to be enforced as if it had been taken by the authorities of the State of enforcement. The actual enforcement takes

74 1996 Convention Practical Handbook, para 10.1.

75 Ibid, para 10.2.

place 'in accordance with the law of the requested State to the extent provided by such law, taking into consideration the best interests of the child.'[76]

From an English perspective, an incoming application for the recognition of a foreign order is dealt with under Part 31 of the Family Procedure Rules (Registration of Orders under the Hague Convention 1996). Part 31.4, which provides that:

> (1) Any interested person may apply to the court for an order that the judgment be registered, recognised or not recognised.
>
> (2) An application for registration, recognition or non-recognition must be–
>
> (a) made to a district judge of the principal registry; and
>
> (b) in the form and supported by the documents and the information required by a practice direction.

So far as incoming cases are concerned, and although these cases related to private law proceedings, high court decision such as *Re U: Recognition and Enforcement of Orders under the 1996 Hague Convention* [2023] EWHC 3494 (Fam) and much previously *Re P (Recognition and Registration of Orders under the 1996 Hague Child Protection Convention)* [2014] EWHC 2845 (Fam) underscore the commitment of English courts to recognize and enforce foreign orders[77] under the 1996 Hague Convention. In *Re U*, the English

---

[76] 1996 Convention, Article 28.

[77] *cf* Albeit a case concerning *Brussels II Revised* (but with relevance to the 1996 Hague Convention) this was evident in *In re M (Children) (Contact: Enforcement of Foreign Order)* [2017] EWCA Civ 891, where

court recognised a French order (of July 2022), and in *Re P* the court granted the father's application for the registration of an Australian order in England. In Re P, The father, residing in Australia, sought to have an order issued by Justice Bennett of the Family Court of Australia recognized and registered in England. This order, made under the Australian Family Law Act 1975, pertained to parental responsibility and child protection measures concerning the child, P. The mother, residing in England, appeared in person during the proceedings. Re U addressed the recognition and enforcement of French child protection orders concerning a child, U, born on 24 March 2019. Following the parents' separation in the summer of 2020, U was placed under the care of French social services due to child protection concerns. On 18 July 2022, the French Children's Court granted supervised access rights to the mother. Subsequently, the father sought recognition and enforcement of the French orders in England, alongside applications for a non-molestation order, a prohibited steps order, and a Section 91(14) order under the Children Act 1989. Conversely, the mother applied for access to U under Article 21 of the 1980 Hague Convention. The court identified two central issues:

> *"25. In essence there are two linked issues before me:*
>
> *i. the father's application for the French orders to be recognized and enforced in this jurisdiction; and*
>
> *ii. whether recognition and enforcement of the French orders should be refused under Article 23 of the 1996 Hague Convention."*

---

the English Court of Appeal ruled that it lacked the authority to require a UK child welfare body to supervise contact as mandated by an Estonian court order, leading to the dismissal of the appeal.

The English High Court recognized and enforced the French orders from July 2022, determining that they should be upheld within the jurisdiction of England and Wales. However, the court found that the September 2022 order had expired based on its wording and was replaced by undertakings given by the mother. Consequently, the court declined to extend or vary the arrangements under the French orders to allow the mother to care for U in France over the summer holidays.

For an incoming case, the jurisdiction of judicial authorities regarding the recognition and enforcement of child protection measures under the 1996 Hague Convention is set out in the 2010 Regulation. Specifically, Regulation 8 of The Parental Responsibility and Measures for the Protection of Children (International Obligations) (England and Wales and Northern Ireland) Regulations 2010 provides that:

> 8.— (1) The High Court has jurisdiction to entertain an application under Article 24 of the Convention for recognition, or non-recognition, of a measure taken in another Contracting State.
>
> (2) But where the recognition or non-recognition of a measure is raised as an incidental question in another court, that court may determine the issue.
>
> (3) The High Court is also to have jurisdiction—
>
> (a) to register a measure taken in another Contracting State for enforcement under Article 26 of the Convention, and
>
> (b) to entertain an application for a declaration—

(i) that a person has, or does not have, parental responsibility for a child by virtue of Article 16 of the Convention, or

(ii) as to the extent of a person's parental responsibility for a child by virtue of that Article.

Further, the High Court has the authority to hear applications under Article 24 of the 1996 Convention for the recognition or non-recognition of child protection measures taken in another State. However, if the issue of recognition arises incidentally in another court, that court may determine the matter. In addition to recognition, the High Court has jurisdiction to register child protection measures from another contracting State for enforcement under Article 26 of the Convention. This ensures that foreign child protection orders can be effectively implemented within England and Wales. The High Court is also responsible for issuing declarations relating to parental responsibility under Article 16 of the Convention. This includes determining whether a person has or does not have parental responsibility for a child and clarifying the extent of such responsibility where necessary. These provisions establish the High Court as the primary authority for cross-border child protection matters while allowing other courts to address recognition issues when they arise in the course of separate proceedings.

In summary, practitioners must first be able to identify when a particular case would benefit from relevant provisions under the 1996 Hague Convention, especially in situations where its use extends beyond an application already underway via ICACU. While the Convention provides a framework for the mutual recognition and enforcement of child protection measures across States, practitioners should be mindful that recognition—whether incoming or outgoing—is by "operation of law" and is largely determined by applying the *lex fori*. Accordingly, any foreign order must align with domestic public policy and, most importantly, serve the child's best interests.

## 5.2 Article 23(2): Grounds for Refusal

Pursuant to Article 23(2), protection of measures may be challenged on six grounds and recognition may be refused.[78] These grounds are "limited and exhaustively enumerated".[79] As such if declaration were to be refused on one of the grounds on which recognition can be denied pursuant to Article 23(2).

> Article 23(2) Recognition may however be refused -
>
> *a)* if the measure was taken by an authority whose jurisdiction was not based on one of the grounds provided for in Chapter II;
>
> *b)* if the measure was taken, except in a case of urgency, in the context of a judicial or administrative proceeding, without the child having been provided the opportunity to be heard, in violation of fundamental principles of procedure of the requested State;
>
> *c)* on the request of any person claiming that the measure infringes his or her parental responsibility, if such measure was taken, except in a case of

---

78 Article 23(2) provides an exhaustive list of the grounds in which recognition may be refused.

79 1996 Convention Practical Handbook, para 13.9

urgency, without such person having been given an opportunity to be heard;

*d)* if such recognition is manifestly contrary to public policy of the requested State, taking into account the best interests of the child;

*e)* if the measure is incompatible with a later measure taken in the non-Contracting State of the habitual residence of the child, where this later measure fulfils the requirements for recognition in the requested State;

*f)* if the procedure provided in Article 33 has not been complied with.

For example, Article 23(2)(b) provides that recognition of a measure can be refused if, except in urgent cases, the child was not given an opportunity to be heard in a way that violates the fundamental procedural principles of the requested State. In essence, the provision allows flexibility in how a child is heard during legal proceedings, recognizing the diversity of legal systems. Further, when a competent authority hears a child, it should document how this was done. If the child is not heard, the decision should reflect that consideration was given and explain why. This aligns with Article 12(2) of the UN Convention on the Rights of the Child but does not mean a child must always be heard. In some cases, such as when both parents agree on the measure, hearing the child may not be necessary. As such, failure to hear the child is only a basis for refusal if it contradicts the core procedural principles of the requested State. This applies equally to judicial and administrative proceedings. However, in urgent cases, procedural requirements should be interpreted more flexibly to ensure timely protection. This provision acts as a safeguard for fair legal procedures while prioritizing the child's best interests. In the child abduction case of *In the Matter of D (A Child) (International Recognition)*,[80] the Court of Appeal addressed the non-recognition of a Romanian court order under the *Brussels IIa Revised Regulation*, based on Article 23 grounds analogous to the 1996 Hague Convention grounds for non-recognition pursuant to Article 23(2). The mother's appeal against the decision to register a Romanian judgment (granting custody to the father) was allowed in the English High Court, on the grounds that the child had not been provided an opportunity to be heard and that the mother had not been properly served. The Court of Appeal upheld non-recognition of the order under Article 23 of the *Brussels IIa Revised Regulation*, reinforcing amongst others, the importance of ensuring that children's rights to participate in proceedings are respected in cross-border child protection matters: -

> "The opportunity for a child to be heard therefore requires an age-appropriate enquiry into his wishes and feelings to enable the decision-maker to understand the child's distinct point of view. The child's entitlement to a voice is a fundamental procedural principle in our system. If he is old enough, it will be his voice and his words. An adult voice will convey the younger child's point of view. Younger children are less able to articulate their wishes, but their feelings may be more vivid than those of older children and of adults, whose views we canvass without a second thought".[81]

80 *In the Matter of D (A Child) (International Recognition)* [2016] EWCA Civ 12

81 Ibid, para 96.

A subsequent appeal to the UK Supreme Court was dismissed,[82] affirming the non-recognition of the Romanian court order under the *Brussels IIa Revised* Regulation. The Supreme Court upheld that the child's right to be heard had been violated, aligning with the Court of Appeal's decision that recognition should be refused under Article 23 due to procedural flaws. This ruling cuts both ways whether dealing with the recognition of a foreign judgment or the making of an English orders intended to stand the test of recognition. The decision emphasizes the importance of ensuring proper procedural safeguards, particularly regarding children's participation in judicial proceedings in cross-border child protection cases.

## 5.3 Article 24: Advanced Recognition

Article 24 provides for an *advance* recognition mechanism whereby any interested person may request a decision (from the competent authorities where the decision is to be recognised and enforced) on the recognition or non-recognition of a foreign measure of protection from another contracting State. Article 24 provides that: -

> Without prejudice to Article 23, paragraph 1, any interested person may request from the competent authorities of a Contracting State that they decide on the recognition or non-recognition of a measure taken in another Contracting State. The procedure is governed by the law of the requested State.

Where measures are taken under Article 23 of the 1996 Hague Convention, and there is a doubt about whether such measures will be recognised by operation of law in another Contracting State, steps could be taken as part of the process of enquiry to seek out recognition

---

82 *In the matter of D (A Child)* [2016] UKSC 34 <http://www.europeanrights.eu/public/sentenze/UKSC22giugno.pdf>

under Article 24. This may involve recognition of an Interim Care Order or Supervision Order in the context of a temporary placement abroad with a prospective kinship carer, but indeed advance recognition may also be sought for custody, contact or relocation provisions,[83] all of which may well fall within the remit of public law proceedings. It is a provision governed by the law of the requested State and whereby, form the perspective of the requesting State, additional safeguards are put in place by utilising advance recognition under Article 24. Given the individualised, unique and prescriptive nature of final care plans (and orders), not least the international variances in concept and terminology, it would be ill-advised to leave it too late and/or make final orders without due diligence either through expert advice on the effectiveness of the proposed orders (ensuring that the orders made will have the same effect and strength as deemed by the UK courts) or an administrative process of advance recognition. Afterall, "it is only at the time when the measure is invoked that a possible dispute over the existence of a ground for non-recognition may be the subject of a ruling"[84] and by then the challenge to recognition may be insurmountable.[85] The Practitioner's Tool on *Cross-Border Recognition and Enforcement of Agreements Reached in the Course of Family Matters involving Children,*[86] though regarding agreements (such as mediated agreements), provides useful insight at paragraph 47:

> To counter any doubts about possible grounds of non-recognition, once the family agreement has been incorporated

---

83 1996 Convention Practical Handbook, para 10.18,13.20.

84 ibid.

85 E.g. *In the matter of D (A Child)* [2016] UKSC 34

86 Permanent Bureau of the HCCH, Practitioner's Tool on *Cross-Border Recognition and Enforcement of Agreements Reached in the Course of Family Matters involving Children*, (The Hague, 2022)

> into a measure of protection, a decision on the recognition or non-recognition of the measure could immediately be sought in the State(s) concerned in accordance with Article 24 of the Child Protection Convention. Depending on the applicable procedural law, a declaration of enforceability or a registration for the purposes of enforcement would have to be obtained if enforcement of the measure of protection is required in the other Contracting Party.

As such, in considering an application for registration under Article 24, practitioners are advised to compile and seek the court's permission in disclosing documents or evidence that demonstrate the following:

1. That the child was given an opportunity to be heard (or in circumstances where this is not possible (e.g., age, urgency), the reasons are properly explained as to the circumstances that led to the child not having the opportunity to be heard and any other relevant factors (for example, that the child was represented);

2. That the judgment is enforceable in the country it was made e.g., England and Wales;

3. Details of the measures taken in England and Wales, specifying the nature and effect of the measure and the date it was taken; for example, an Interim Care Order, Special Guardianship Order, Child Arrangements Order, Specific Issue Order etc;

4. If not apparent from a copy of the judgment, a statement of the grounds upon which the court gave judgment in the English jurisdiction, together with any documentary evidence (for example, threshold document – there may be a preference

for including threshold as a Schedule to be attached to the substantive order);

5. Where appropriate, evidence that Article 33 of the Convention has been complied with, as well as evidence of consent from relevant authorities;

6. An address within the jurisdiction of the court for service of process on the party making the application and the name, address, and place of service in respect of others concerned (typically the respondents).

# CHAPTER SIX

# PRACTICAL EFFECTS OF 1996 HAGUE CONVENTION ORDERS

The 1996 Hague Convention's provisions are designed to facilitate the efficient recognition and enforcement of child protection measures in practice. Given its cross-border nature, it is essential to understand the implications of such orders.

## 6.1 Binding Findings of Fact

Article 25 establishes that authorities in the requested State must accept the factual findings on which the original jurisdiction was based, preventing unnecessary re-litigation. This may include decisions pertaining to the assessments of habitual residence and the child's best interests. It is expected there such findings, taken by judicial authorities in this jurisdiction, clearly outline the facts supporting their decisions.

## 6.2 Enforcement Across Jurisdictions

Article 26 applies when a measure taken in one contracting State "require"[87] enforcement in another. If enforcement is not required, recognition under Article 23 is enough for the measure to take effect.[88]

---

87 Article 26(1) 1996 Hague Convention

88 Explanatory Report, para 132.

The process for declaring enforceability and/or registering a measure is generally outlined by each contracting State and updated as part of the HCCH's preliminary document questionnaires submitted prior to Special Commission meetings.[89] However, these documents may lack a full response, meaning that practitioners typically need to collaborate with relevant authorities and experts to understand the specific details in individual cases. Under Article 26(1) of the 1996 Hague Convention, measures taken in one contracting State shall be "declared enforceable or registered" for enforcement in another State upon request by an interested party, following that receiving State's *lex fori*. The receiving State follows its own legal procedures to declare the measure enforceable or register it for enforcement. Given the distinction between member States who may offer registration or enforceability declaration as an administrative process and those who may require judicial oversight initiated by a lawyer in that State, practitioners may require expert advice to navigate the appropriate process.

Article 26(2) further mandates that this process be "simple and rapid," though it allows each State to determine how to implement this requirement without imposing a specific timeframe. Again, practitioners would benefit from expert advice where State process and consequently timescales are not entirely clear. Though a simple and

89 Permanent Bureau of the HCCH, 'Questionnaire concerning the practical operation of the 1996 Child Protection Convention (Prel. Doc. No 2 of October 2022', (The Hague, 2022). See Country responses to questions 16 and 17: "Declaration of enforceability or registration for the purpose of enforcement (Arts 26, 27 and 28" Available at: <https://www.hcch.net/en/instruments/conventions/specialised-sections/child-protection>

rapid process is envisaged, much still depends on a specific procedure in each contracting State, which may vary from State to State.[90]

Article 26(2) envisages that the procedure of declaration of enforceability and registration, which is governed by the law of the State of enforcement, must be 'simple and rapid'. With the requirement for exequatur long since abolished under the Brussels regime, *Brussels IIa Recast Regulation*[91] carries that principle in ensuring automatic recognition and enforcement of child protection judgments (e.g., final judgments and court settlements) across the EU. This reform seeks to eliminate delays, reduces costs, and enhances cross-border cooperation, promoting swift implementation of decisions in the child's best interests. This notable variance in applying the 1996 Hague Convention as opposed to the circulation of orders pursuant *Brussels IIa Recast Regulation* amongst our European counterparts cannot go amiss.

### 6.3 No Reassessment of Merits

This provision underscores that while procedural reviews may be necessary, the merits of an order cannot be reassessed in the requested State. Together, these provisions promote legal certainty, reduce delays, and enhance cross-border cooperation, ensuring that child

---

90 Permanent Bureau of the HCCH, 'Questionnaire concerning the practical operation of the 1996 Child Protection Convention (Prel. Doc. No 2 of October 2022', (The Hague, 2022). See Country responses to question 16.

91 Article 30: "A decision given in a Member State shall be recognised in the other Member States without any special procedure being required"

protection decisions are implemented swiftly and effectively in the best interests of the child.

# CHAPTER SEVEN

# ALTERNATIVE CARE ABROAD

## 7.1 Article 33

When an authority considers placing a child in foster care, institutional care, or under *kafala* or a similar arrangement in another contracting State, the Convention imposes strict procedural requirements. These safeguards must be met before the placement can be legally implemented. As such, a fundamental role of the 1996 Hague Convention is to secure and ensure the best interests of children in cross-border placements as outlined in Article 33: –

(1) If an authority having jurisdiction under Articles 5 to 10 contemplates the placement of the child in a foster family or institutional care, or the provision of care by *kafala* or an analogous institution, and if such placement or such provision of care is to take place in another Contracting State, it shall first consult with the Central Authority or other competent authority of the latter State. To that effect it shall transmit a report on the child together with the reasons for the proposed placement or provision of care.

(2) The decision on the placement or provision of care may be made in the requesting State only if the Central Authority or other competent authority of the requested State has consented to the placement or provision of care, taking into account the child's best interests.

Article 33, when read in conjunction with Articles 3(e) and 23(2)(f), establishes a framework for regulating the placement of children outside their family in another country, ensuring appropriate legal oversight and protection. Considered as "only basic rules",[92] it serves as a foundational framework for States to build upon, yet, paradoxically, this flexibility has led to a lack of settled practice among contracting States. One of the key ambiguities concerns which child protection measures fall under Article 33 and thus require compliance with its procedural safeguards. A major point of contention is whether placing a child with extended family members—such as grandparents, aunts, or uncles—qualifies as a placement requiring Article 33 procedures. The Eighteenth Diplomatic Session[93] did not provide a definitive answer, and this lack of clarity has led to divergent interpretations among legal experts and authorities. Indeed, In the past, previous Special Commission meetings[94] highlighted these challenges, with experts divided on the potential consequences of including or excluding such placements under Article 33. Some argued that requiring formal procedures for placing children with extended family abroad would create unnecessary bureaucratic obstacles, potentially delaying or complicating beneficial family reunifications.[95] Others, however, expressed concern that without Article 33 safeguards, the receiving State might be unaware of critical

92 1996 Convention Practical Handbook, para 13.38.

93 1996 Convention Practical Handbook, para 13.37 referring to Minutes No 16 of the *Proceedings of the Eighteenth Session* concerning the more developed Work Doc. No.89.

94 Permanent Bureau of the HCCH, Conclusions and Recommendations and Report of Part I of the Sixth Meeting of the Special Commission on the Practical Operation of the 1980 Hague Child Abduction Convention and the 1996 Hague Child Protection Convention (The Hague, 2011) para 172

95 1996 Convention Practical Handbook, para 13.37013.38.

details about the child's background, such as prior child protection concerns, immigration issues, or access to essential public services.[96] This could result in inadequate oversight, leaving the child vulnerable in the receiving country. Moreover, if Article 33 does not apply to placements with extended family, there is a risk that some cross-border child placements could bypass necessary legal scrutiny, potentially leading to situations where children are placed in environments that have not been adequately assessed. This raises broader concerns about ensuring ongoing monitoring and protection of children in alternative care settings. Ultimately, the lack of settled practice means that different jurisdictions handle these cases inconsistently. While the original intent behind Article 33 was to provide procedural safeguards for international child placements—mirroring aspects of the 1993 Hague Intercountry Adoption Convention—the absence of clear guidelines has led to uncertainty. Until there is further clarification, either through international consensus or legal precedent, the practical application of Article 33 may continue to pose challenges for child welfare authorities and courts.

In 2023, the HCCH Eighth Special Commission Meeting explored,[97] *inter-alia*, issues regarding the cross-border placement of children in alternative care as regards to the 1996 Hague Convention:

> XX. Placement or provision of care of the child in another Contracting Party under Articles 3(e) and 33 of the 1996 Child Protection Convention

---

96 Ibid.

97 SC Eight Meeting, Conclusions and Recommendations' paras 82-90. The SC has recommended that the Permanent Bureau gather more information on Article 33 from Contracting Parties and establish a Working Group to develop a model form for cooperation and a guide on its operation.

[...]

2. Scope of Articles 3(e) and 33 of the 1996 Child Protection Convention

83 The SC agreed that the placement of the child in a foster family or in institutional care, or the provision of care by kafala or an analogous institution (i.e., alternative care arrangements) that fall under the scope of Articles 3(e) and 33 of the 1996 Child Protection Convention are measures of 14 protection decided by a competent authority (i.e., judicial or administrative authority (e.g., a government youth and welfare agency, a social worker)) to protect and assist children who are usually temporarily or permanently deprived of their family environment, or cannot remain in their family environment as it would not be in their best interests. In a cross-border context, the SC understood that the two States involved in the placement (i.e., the requesting State (State of origin) and the requested State (receiving State)) share the responsibility to protect and assist the child, which explains the mandatory nature of the consultation provided for under Article 33.

84 The SC noted that purely private arrangements resulting in an informal care placement do not fall within the scope of Article 33, as such placements are not decided by a competent authority.

85 The SC noted that a child travelling abroad for tourism purposes with their foster parent from their State of habitual residence is not a placement abroad and, therefore, does not fall within the scope of Article 33.

> 86 The SC further noted that the authority of a person who has the care of a child in particular circumstances, such as when they are attending school or a summer camp abroad, would be covered under Article 3(d).
>
> 87 Considering that, in general, notaries reflect and give legal validity to the wishes of the party(ies) in private agreements or unilateral acts, they would not be considered a "competent authority" deciding a measure of alternative care. Therefore, the SC further noted that private arrangements in the form of an agreement or unilateral act, including a notarial kafala, validated by a notary do not fall within the scope of Article 33.
>
> 88 The SC noted that, in several States, relatives have to be eligible and suitable in accordance with the law to provide alternative care.
>
> 89 The SC noted the possibility for competent authorities to make use of Article 34 to request information relevant to possible measures of protection of the child, if the situation of the child so requires, under the Convention. Authorities are encouraged to consider making use of Article 34 in preparation for a request under Article 33.

The discussions reaffirmed the procedural safeguards required under Article 33 and clarified its scope in relation to different care arrangements. One key finding was the mandatory consultation process between the requesting State (the child's country of origin) and the receiving State (where the child is to be placed). Before a child can be placed in alternative care abroad, the competent authority of the requesting State must consult the relevant authority in the receiving State. This involves discussing the feasibility of the placement, sharing a report on the child, and explaining the reasons for seeking care outside the country of origin. The receiving State must then formally consent before the requesting State can issue a final decision on the placement.

Deliberations at the Eight Special Commission Meeting confirmed that alternative care arrangements, such as placement in foster families, institutional care, or *kafala*, fall under Articles 3(e) and 33 of the Convention. These measures are intended to protect children who cannot remain in their family environment, whether temporarily or permanently. Given that both the requesting and receiving States share responsibility for the child's protection, formal consultation and approval are essential. However, the Special Commission clarified that private care arrangements—where a child is informally placed with relatives or caregivers without a formal decision from a competent authority—do not fall under Article 33. Similarly, short-term travel, such as a foster child going on holiday with their foster parent, does not constitute an international placement requiring consultation. In cases where a child is staying abroad for schooling or summer camps, these situations are covered under Article 3(d) rather than Article 33.

Should practitioners find themselves dealing with a case that involves a cross border private arrangement requiring legal recognition, at the Eight Special Commission Meeting, it was further clarified that notarial acts, such as notarial *kafala*, do not qualify as measures under Article 33.[98] Since notaries primarily formalize private agreements rather than making protective decisions as a competent authority, such arrangements remain outside the Convention's scope. However, in some jurisdictions, relatives providing alternative care must meet legal eligibility criteria, reinforcing the need for proper oversight in family placements. Finally, recommendations of the Special Commission encouraged authorities to make use of Article 34, which allows them to request additional information relevant to child protection before

[98] SC Eight Meeting, Conclusions and Recommendations' para 87.

initiating a formal request under Article 33. This provision helps ensure that all necessary legal and welfare considerations are taken into account before a cross-border placement decision is made.

## 7.2 Mandatory Consultation

Practitioners, particularly those representing the Applicant or leading enquiries under the 1996 Hague Convention, must ensure that the mandatory consultation process outlined in Article 33 is fully adhered to. This compliance is crucial for the effective handling of the cases and to avoid non-recognition concerns. The starting point, if in doubt, is to consult with the Central Authority of the requested State (through ICACU where possible) when contemplating a cross-border placement to check whether Article 33 protocol is engaged. The determination of whether Article 33 applies will depend on the requested State's assessment of the nature of the proposed placement and its compatibility with national laws.

The procedure involves the following minimum steps:

*(i) disusing the potential for such a placement;*

*(ii) transmitting a report on the child, outlining their personal circumstances, care needs, and any relevant background information;*

*(iii) The reasons for the proposed placement or provision of care, explaining why the specific placement is considered beneficial for the child.*

This ensures that the receiving State has the necessary information to assess whether the placement is appropriate and complies with its national laws and child protection standards. Each contracting State has the option to designate a specific authority to handle these requests. If such a designation is made, it is published on the HCCH's website.[99] In some jurisdiction, there isn't a standard template for reports pursuant to Article 33. However, there may well be additional steps beyond the administrative process, e.g., the oversight of a judicial authority. In Poland, for example, the application will be considered by a Guardianship court where it is open for the court to request professional opinion before consenting to the Article 33 application.[100] Such report would include consideration of whether the proposed placement is in the best interest of the child.

As such, a child's placement cannot proceed unless the Central Authority or another competent authority in the receiving State formally consents to it.[101] The decision must take into account the child's best interests, ensuring that the placement will provide adequate care, stability, and protection. This requirement serves as an important safeguard, preventing children from being moved to another country without the necessary legal and welfare assessments. If the receiving country does not consent, the placement may not be recognized under the 1996 Hague Convention. According to a CFAB case audit of 200 cases, it was found that in 23 of the 100 child protection cases audited, it was not possible to ensure that the child

99 1996 Hague Convention: Specialised Section: Authorities. Available at <https://www.hcch.net/en/instruments/conventions/authorities1/?cid=70>

100 See Article 35a of the "2011 Act": Journal Laws of 2011 No. 149 item 887 ACT of June 9, 2011, on family support and the foster care system (Dz. U. 2011 Nr 149 poz. 887 U S T AWA z dnia 9 czerwca 2011 r. o wspieraniu rodziny i systemie pieczy zastępczej); reinforced by the Polish Code of Civil Procedure.

101 Explanatory Report, para 127.

was safe when the child had travelled to another country.[102] This provision protects children from being placed in inappropriate or unsafe environments and ensures that their rights and welfare are prioritized. Such failures could lead to delays, disputes, and instability, which can be highly disruptive to a child's life and well-being. Further, with Article 33 consent, the possibility of non-recognition pursuant to Article 23(2) is diminished, if not eliminated.

[102] CFAB, 'Cross-border child safeguarding: Challenges, effective social work practice and outcomes for children' (2018) para 5.2.1

# CHAPTER EIGHT

# PROTECTIVE MEASURES IN CHILD ABDUCTION CASES

A key interaction arising between the two Conventions is when protective measures, urgent or otherwise, are required within a 1980 Hague Convention case; or when the 1980 Hague Convention is invoked because a wrongful removal/retention occurs during proceedings. Further, a child abduction case under the 1980 Hague Convention may intersect with child protection issues that engage the local authority. Such situations may arise in cases where the local authority shares parental responsibility and has initiated proceedings, or where concerns uncovered during an application for rights of access under Article 21 lead to the involvement of the local authority. The 1996 Hague Convention supports[103] the1980 Hague Convention by providing jurisdictional clarity and substantive child protective measures in the child's State of habitual residence. The 1996 Convention Practical Handbook[104] highlights the Convention's role in parental disputes over custody and access (Article 21 of the 1980 Convention) and cases of international abduction. Note that while the 1996 Hague Convention does not explicitly reference the 1980 Hague

---

103 Thorpe LJ in *Re Y (A Child) (Abduction: Undertakings Given for Return of Child)* [2013] EWCA Civ 129 [9]. It is also said to have inspired some of the rules under Brussels II *bis*, such as Article 15: Thalia Kruger and Liselot Samyn, "Brussels II bis: Successes and Suggested Improvements" (2016) 12 Journal of Private International Law 132 at 150 discussing the interaction between Brussels II *bis* and the 1996 Convention.

104 The 1996 Convention Practical Handbook, para 1.2

Convention beyond Article 7 and Article 50, it affirms the primacy of the Child Abduction Convention while asserting its own jurisdictional powers in securing the return of abducted children. As outlined by the HCCH, the 1996 Hague Convention reinforces the 1980 Convention:

> "The Child Protection Convention reinforces the 1980 Child Abduction Convention by underlining the primary role played by the authorities of the child's habitual residence in deciding the matters that affect the child in the long term. It also adds to the efficacy of any urgent protective measures ordered by a judge when returning a child to their State of habitual residence (Art. 11). These protective measures lapse as soon as the authorities of the child's State of habitual residence have taken the measures required by the situation (Art. 11(2))."[105]

When contemplating protective measures in abduction cases,[106] it is important to assess their adequacy and enforceability in the child's

---

105 Outline, HCCH 1996 Child Protection Convention <https://assets.hcch.net/docs/be4083a2-ed90-4dc2-bb97-13be22e6a5d8.pdf>

106 O Momoh, *A Practical Guide to International Parental Child Abduction Law: England and Wales* (Law Brief Publishing 2023), chapter 5.3.5. See also K Trimmings, O Momoh, I Callander 'Protection of Abducting Mothers in Return Proceedings: Intersection between Domestic Violence and Parental Child Abduction: UK National Report' (2019) EU funded report. This report was funded by the European Union's Rights, Equality and Citizenship Programme (2014-2020); POAM Project Team, *Best Practice Guide: Protection of Abducting Mothers in Return Proceedings: Intersection between domestic violence and parental child abduction* (2020) POAM Project; O Momoh, 'The need for cross-border protective measures in return proceedings' in Trimmings K, Dutta A, Honorati C and Zupan M

State of habitual residence. Each case must be evaluated individually, taking into account, *inter-alia,* the specific circumstances of the child's protection needs. Further, should the court approve measures of protection attached to return orders, practitioners should ensure that the measures are drafted in terms that align with equivalent protections in the child's habitual residence, either be incorporated into the return order or explicitly set as conditions for return. If concerns remain over enforcement, again, Article 24 of the 1996 Hague Convention can be utilised to seek advance recognition. Alternatively, seeking out mirroring orders in the requesting State before a return order comes into effect may provide further security, as seen in *Re Y (A Child).*[107]

(eds), *Domestic Violence and Parental Child Abduction* (1st edn, Intersentia 2022).

107 *Re Y (A Child) (Abduction: Undertakings Given for Return of Child)* [2013] EWCA Civ 129. Following *Re Y*, authorities that have shown the High Court's utility of the 1996 Hague Convention, such as *RD v DB* [2015] EWHC 1817 (Fam), *In the matter of A (A Child) (Hague Abduction; Art 13(b): Protective Measures)* [2019] EWHC 649 (Fam) and *In the Matter of S O D*, High Court, 31 January 2019 (unreported). Of course, in non-Convention cases, obtaining expert reports on recognition and enforcement procedures in that country is often necessary.

# CHAPTER NINE

# THE PLACEMENT OF CHILDREN ABROAD UNDER THE AUSPICES OF: SPECIAL GUARDIANSHIP ORDERS, CHILD ARRANGEMENTS ORDERS, ORDERS CONFERRING OR LIMITING PARENTAL RESPONSIBILITY, OTHER PUBLIC LAW ORDERS

## 9.1 The Role of National and Foreign Authorities

Under the 1996 Hague Convention, several authorities play key roles in child protection cases. Central Authorities, designated by each contracting State, are primarily responsible for implementing the Convention's provisions. Additionally, other "competent authorities", such as "judicial" or "administrative authorities", "public authorities" or designated "bodies", may be involved to facilitate the cooperation and communication necessary to protect the child. Entities authorised by Central Authorities to assist with tasks or facilitating communication. These authorities, working collaboratively across borders, can request or provide information regarding the child's situation and take necessary protective actions. Each contracting State may also appoint more than one Central Authority, depending on its legal structure. In cases involving the placement of children abroad under the auspices of Special Guardianship Orders, Child Arrangements Orders, or other public law orders, the role of public and other designated bodies becomes crucial. For instance, Article 32 of the 1996 Hague Convention establishes the framework for cooperation between contracting States in matters of child protection enables a request for assistance from a State with which the child has a substantial connection,[108] such as a former habitual residence, where family members live who are willing to look after the child, where a parent with access or contact rights resides or a State where the child has extended family members that are visited frequently. This operation of Article 32 is consistent with the guidance under the 1996 Convention Practical Handbook.[109] Furthermore, the request must include detailed "reasons",[110] explaining why it is necessary for the child's protection. Returning to the role of a Central Authority, requests for cooperation should be submitted to the Central Authority in the child's habitual residence and current location. Upon receipt, the Central Authority may either handle the request itself or delegate the task to a public authority or another body. However, the requested Central Authority is not obligated to act; it has the discretion to respond directly or through designated authorities. This ensures flexibility while maintaining a structured approach to the process.

## 9.2 European Placements and Cross-border Legal Considerations

Aspects of the challenges arising from cross-border child placements, both temporary and permanent, under the 1996 Hague Convention are explored, focusing on three frameworks: Special Guardianship Orders, Child Arrangements Orders, and Interim Care Orders. Note that this section does not examine final Care Orders, as it would be highly unusual for a court to approve one with the plan for placing a child aboard, even when Article 33 is invoked. If such circumstances

---

108 The connecting factor "substantial connection" is reference under Articles 8, 15, 32 and 47.

109 1996 Convention Practical Handbook, para 11.24.

110 Article 32. The term "detailed" reasons is introduced in the 1996 Convention Practical Handbook.

arise during proceedings, jurisdiction should typically be transferred, as social and/or children's services in the receiving jurisdiction would become significantly involved and need to assume effective parental responsibility. The complexities that emerge when these orders are applied in jurisdictions with differing legal frameworks and terminology are examined, with practical guidance provided to practitioners navigating these issues.

### 9.2.1 Special Guardianship Order

A common issue under the 1996 Hague Convention arises when an order includes provisions that have no direct equivalent in the requested State and vice versa. For example, in many jurisdictions there is no direct equivalent to a Section 14A (Children Act 1989) Special Guardianship Order which grants parental responsibility to a person other than the child's parent. The nearest equivalent may be to confer parental rights and responsibility and/or as a consequence "guardianship" status on the alternative carer or some other form of kinship/family foster care. For many, there are also complexities around the imposition of a hierarchy of parental responsibility as a special guardianship order would entail. In this regard, a carefully formulated equivalence of a special guardianship order might range from an order conferring parental responsibility or sole custody or guardianship, to mention but a few.

In example, a kinship placement of a child under the auspices of an English "special guardianship order" in Poland would be considered a *family* foster care placement (distinguishable from *institutional* foster care). The divergence in legal definitions and procedural requirements between different jurisdictions means that practitioners should not only seek expert advice, but ensure that at the conclusion of the process, any final order adopts mutual language where possible. For example, referring to 1996 Hague Convention terminology such as 'rights', 'powers' and 'responsibilities' (Art 1(2) 1996 Hague Convention). National provisions do not confer parental responsibility in the manner that English law does. Rather, it vests obligations, duties, and rights to carry out regular custody over the child which would include his upbringing (Art 112 Polish FGC).[111] Nevertheless, the issue of creating a hierarchy of parental rights may be addressed by an accompanying provision within the order *limiting* the parental responsibility of the parents (e.g. measures akin to a Prohibited Steps Order). Thus, in achieving the essence of an SGO under English law and leaning on the concept of parental responsibility in so far as is possible, it is only appropriate that for the avoidance of doubt the order expressly recites the definition of Special Guardianship under English law (in particular its effect pursuant to section 14 C (1) CA1989). Thereafter, in reconciling with the position in law in the receiving State, indicate the intention that the status granted to the special guardians is intended to confer rights, duties, powers, responsibilities, and authority in relation to the child and his property (section 3(1) CA 1989).

---

111 Unofficial translated version of the Family and Guardianship Code produced in Kosior W J, and Lukasiewicz J M (2018) *Family Law in Poland*, Legal Publishing House, Rzeszow < https://open.icm.edu.pl/server/api/core/bitstreams/04cf4e81-a243-4fbc-aa09-fdbbbecd1ef4/content>

### 9.2.2 Child Arrangements Order

Similarly, the term "Child Arrangements Order" (CAO) represents a linguistic particularity[112] unique to the legal framework of England and Wales which does not appear as a distinct legal concept in the domestic laws of other contracting States to the 1996 Hague Convention. While the CAO governs situations concerning a child's living and contact arrangements, other jurisdictions may regulate comparable matters under broader parental responsibility frameworks without an equivalent statutory designation. As such, even though the concept of parental responsibility in other contracting States generally aligns with the definition provided under English law at section 3(1) of the Children Act 1989—encompassing all rights, duties, powers, responsibilities, and authority exercised by a parent in relation to a child and their property— specific terminology and legal constructs vary. For example, under the Norwegian 1981 Children Act, residence is regulated under the term 'custody' (chapter 5), while contact is referred to as "access" (chapter 6). Even joint parental responsibility (section 37) is conceptually distinct from sole custody (section 36). Consequently, when seeking recognition of a CAO outside England and Wales as a means of placing a child in the protective care of the proposed carer, it is essential to frame the order using universally understood treaty terminology, such as "parental responsibility" and "sole custody", as articulated in the 1996 Hague Convention. Accordingly, as with an SGO, this divergence underscores the necessity for practitioners to interpret and apply cross-border measures in accordance with the substantive rights conferred rather than the specific terminology used in domestic legislation.

112 Explanatory Report, para 20.

### 9.2.3 Interim Care Order

When considering the temporary placement of a child abroad under an Interim Care Order (ICO) in England and Wales, following a positive viability assessment, the process will largely depend on whether advance recognition under Article 24 or consultations under Article 33 of the 1996 Hague Convention have already taken place. These steps typically lay the foundation for further liaison with foreign authorities, collaborating across a spectrum from the delegation of temporary powers to post-placement support upon final resolution. If such considerations are at an early stage, it is still expected that the Local Authority or another relevant body has engaged with social services, child protection agencies or designated court officials in the receiving State to assess the kinship placement.[113] To ensure legal clarity and international cooperation, the order accompanying the temporary placement should explicitly state that it is made pursuant to the 1996 Hague Convention (Articles 1, 11, 23(1), and 26) and constitutes a measure of protection taken in England and Wales, to be recognised by operation of law in the receiving contracting State.

The English court retains jurisdiction over the child until final orders are made, ensuring continued oversight. However, even with an ICO, without consent from all parties with parental responsibility or a specific court order granting permission for temporary or permanent removal from the jurisdiction, international placement may present legal challenges. To facilitate placement with identified kinship carers, such as the child's grandparents, a legal framework must be established that ensures both recognition and enforceability of the interim arrangements. One possible approach is for the court to grant an Interim Child Arrangements Order (Live With Order)[114] in favour of

---

113 See Chapter 12 on Guidance and Collaborations.

114 Explore in conjunction with observations at 9.2.2.

the proposed carers. This would confer parental responsibility on the grandparents while maintaining the Local Authority's statutory role under the ICO. If not already, the Local Authority must also assess the receiving State's legal position on recognising such interim measures pursuant to the 1996 Hague Convention, ensuring that the child's placement is not only lawful but also enforceable within the host country's jurisdiction.

Best practice in international placements highlights the importance of collaborative working with foreign authorities.[115] This would involve engaging with child welfare agencies to coordinate assessments or, where appropriate, inviting the proposed carers to England for a comprehensive evaluation by home social workers. In some cases, social workers abroad may be better positioned to undertake viability and full kinship assessments, provided they possess the necessary legal authorisation and match the standards expected in the English courts. Apart from seeking out expert advice, the involvement of embassies may further facilitate communication with relevant authorities, assist in locating additional family members, and provide guidance on applicable child protection laws.

Additionally, immigration considerations must be addressed at an early stage. For example, if the placement is contemplated in an EU member State or Schengen area, British nationals may enter visa-free for up to 90 days (in a 180-day period) within the Schengen area,[116] of course this is contingent on conditions such as proof of return travel and accommodation. If the intended placement is to extend beyond

---

115 Department of Education, '*Woking with Foreign Authorities: Child Protection Cases and Care Orders: Departmental advice for local authorities, social workers, service managers and children's services lawyers*', July 2014

116 "*Travelling to the EU and Schengen area*" *<https://www.gov.uk/travel-to-eu-schengen-area>*

this period or transition into a permanent arrangement, specialist immigration advice should be sought to determine whether a long-stay visa or residency permit is required. The Local Authority should also explore contingency planning in case of placement breakdown.

### 9.3 Recommended Measures in Ensuring Effectiveness of Orders

To ensure the best possible chance of recognition and enforcement of outgoing orders made in England and Wales, which may include orders pursuant to advanced recognition or in some instances mirror orders, the following non-exhaustive measures are recommended as a starting point:

(i) Where a Child Arrangements Order (CAO) or Special Guardianship Order (SGO) is granted, the order should include a declaration stating that it constitutes a "measure" for the purposes of Article 23(1) of the 1996 Hague Convention.

(ii) The order should recite that the SGO/ CAO is made with the intention of conferring parental responsibility, aligning with the legal framework of the receiving jurisdiction. The SGO/CAO should be framed to reflect equivalent terminology under the law of the receiving State while maintaining its intended legal effect.

(iii) The Local Authority should consider covering any fees arising from the Article 26 application in relation to the child(ren), whether for a CAO or SGO, as well as any registration costs incurred in the receiving jurisdiction. For example, the registration of the order in the local court of the requested State (Article 29 of the 1996 Hague Convention) may be a necessary step that requires funding.

(iv) An application for permanent removal from the jurisdiction should be heard alongside the final hearing, with an appropriate court order issued to that effect. This ensures compliance with the procedural requirements of both the requesting and receiving States, preventing jurisdictional conflicts.

(v) The order should include recitals or an attached schedule reflecting the position of all relevant parties, including the recognition of parental responsibility granted under the SGO/CAO.

(vi) The order should also acknowledge the jurisdictional transition to the receiving State upon the child's placement, in accordance with Articles 16 and 17 of the 1996 Hague Convention.

(vii) Where an SGO is granted, while the substantive order should reference the proposed child arrangements (contact), a separate CAO setting out the parties' mutual expectations for contact should be affixed as a schedule to the substantive order. In addition, any contact order issued should be endorsed as having been made for the purpose of recognition and enforcement in the requesting State under Articles 23-28 of the 1996 Hague Child Protection Convention.

## 9.4 Guardian ad Litem

No discussion of child protection law is complete without acknowledging the voice of the child. In public law proceedings, a guardian plays a crucial role in representing and safeguarding the child's welfare. In England and Wales, Cafcass appoints guardians under the Children Act 1989, ensuring that the child's rights, needs, and best interests are at the centre of any legal process. Section 41 of the Children Act 1989 (complimented by Rule 16.4 of the Family Procedure Rules 2010) provides that-

> 41 [Representation of child]
>
> (1) or the purpose of any specified proceedings,[117] the court shall appoint [an officer of the Service] or a Welsh family proceedings officer] for the child concerned unless satisfied that it is not necessary to do so in order to safeguard his interests.

A children's guardian is automatically appointed in public law care proceedings to represent the child's best interests. Specific proceedings defined under section 41(6) include an application for a care or supervision order. This is mandated to ensure independent representation, particularly when decisions about the child's welfare, such as removal from the family, are being made. In private law proceedings, Rule 16.4 of the Family Procedure Rules 2010 provides the framework for the appointment of a guardian, though it is not automatic and depends on the circumstances of the case, typically when the child's welfare or interests are at significant risk. Indeed, Rule 16.4 allows the court to appoint a guardian in private law proceedings where it considers that a child requires independent representation.

In international cases under the 1996 Hague Convention, where cross-border complexities can significantly impact a child's future, a guardian ensures that the child's voice is heard. The guardian assists the court in understanding the child's views, emotional well-being, overall best interests, and any relevant risk assessments. This is especially true in cases involving placement in another country,

---

117 See section 41(6) Children Act 1989.

jurisdictional transfers, or cross-border care proceedings. where a child may feel uncertain or distressed about their future. In cases where a court is deciding whether to transfer jurisdiction under Articles 8 and 9 of the 1996 Hague Convention, a guardian provides crucial insights into how a change in legal authority may affect the child's stability and well-being. Similarly, if a child is at risk and urgent protective measures are needed under Article 11, the guardian plays a key role in advising whether immediate intervention is necessary. In cases where the recognition of orders is contested under Article 23, the role of the guardian becomes even more pronounced. If a protective measure is refused recognition in another State, the guardian may need to advocate for alternative legal remedies to ensure the child's safety and welfare. Similarly, in instances of alternative care abroad, the child's perspective should be central to decision-making, reinforcing the necessity of child-focused legal representation. Ultimately, the guardian ensures that the child is not lost in legal complexities and that their rights, safety, and well-being remain the priority, whether in domestic care proceedings or international legal disputes under the 1996 Hague Convention.

## 9.5 Divergent Concepts and Terminology

In cross-border cases, divergent concepts and terminology are to be expected, as previously explored with regard to Child Arrangements Orders and Special Guardianship Orders. One particularly relevant legal term in this context is “parental responsibility”. Article 1 of the 1996 Hague Convention defines "parental responsibility" as encompassing parental authority or any analogous relationship determining the rights, powers, and responsibilities of parents, guardians, or other legal representatives concerning a child's person and property. This broad and inclusive definition ensures that diverse legal frameworks across contracting States recognize and uphold the rights and duties of those responsible for a child's care and protection.

It extends beyond biological parents to include guardians and other legal representatives, fostering international consistency in child protection matters and facilitating cross-border cooperation in custody, guardianship, and care arrangements.

However, significant variations exist across jurisdictions regarding the scope of parental responsibility. While some legal systems interpret it comprehensively—covering legal and practical aspects such as education, healthcare, and religious upbringing—others adopt a narrower approach, focusing primarily on legal authority and decision-making rights. These differences pose challenges in cross-border cases, particularly in determining the extent of parental authority and enforcing parental rights and obligations across legal systems. It is hoped that future projects will involve the development of a comprehensive lexicon of terminology and concepts, aimed at bridging these gaps and providing relevant stakeholders with a solid foundation for addressing conflict of law issues.

# CHAPTER TEN

# UNACCOMPANIED MINORS

Among the categories of children who stand to benefit from the implementation of the 1996 Convention are refugees and unaccompanied minors. Indeed, unaccompanied minors may become subject to care proceedings or come under the responsibility of the Local Authority for various reasons. The 1996 Hague Convention provides a crucial legal framework for addressing the protection needs of unaccompanied minors in cross-border situations whether due to conflict, displacement, or trafficking, who often face heightened vulnerabilities in international situations. By clarifying which State holds jurisdiction over their protection, the Convention ensures that these children receive timely and appropriate care, rather than being left in legal limbo. The Special Commission has acknowledged the importance of the Convention in this context, thanking States and organizations for their contributions and welcoming the participation of the Permanent Bureau in the Consultation Group on Children of Ukraine under the Council of Europe.[118] In 2024, the Permanent Bureau published an updated handbook on *the Application of the 1996 Child Protection Convention to Unaccompanied and Separated Children*.[119] The handbook provides guidance on implementing the

[118] This group focuses on private international law issues related to the 1996 Convention, highlighting its relevance in the protection of children affected by crisis situations, including unaccompanied minors.

[119] Permanent Bureau of the HCCH, The Application of the 1996 Child Protection Convention to Unaccompanied And Separated Children, (The Hague, 2024). Available at <https://assets.hcch.net/docs/96a3875d-fb7c-44dc-99b0-844c39562851.pdf>

1996 Hague Convention, its scope and applicability to children without parental care, including refugees and those displaced internationally. Amongst others, meriting attention is the consideration to be given to the careful assessment of the best interests of children on a case-by-case basis (in transfer of jurisdiction matters).[120] The document outlines jurisdictional rules, detailing which authorities are competent to take protective measures, and discusses applicable law provisions. It also highlights mechanisms for international cooperation among contracting States to ensure the protection of vulnerable children. Annexes offer practical examples and scenarios to illustrate the Convention's application in various contexts.

A key challenge in protecting unaccompanied minors under international law is determining their habitual residence. Article 6 of the 1996 Convention acknowledges situations where a child's habitual residence cannot be easily established.[121] This can occur when a child moves frequently between States or is abandoned, making it difficult to gather the necessary evidence to determine where the child is habitually resident. In such cases, the Convention allows authorities to apply alternative jurisdictional rules, ensuring that legal protections are not hindered by technical difficulties in establishing residency.[122]

The Convention also includes provisions for sharing critical information about children in danger.[123] Article 36 stipulates that when a child is exposed to serious risk, the competent authorities of the State responsible for the child's protection must notify the authorities of any other State where the child has moved or is

---

120 Ibid, section 2.3.4.

121 Ibid, section 2.3.3 and 2.3.4.

122 Ibid, see also Annex 2.

123 Ibid, para 56-57, Annex Ib, page 39, 46, 56.

present.[124] This is particularly relevant for unaccompanied minors who may be fleeing dangerous situations or in need of urgent intervention. The Explanatory Report of the Convention provides examples of situations where children may be deemed at serious risk, including cases where a measure of protection is required as a result of "*his or her presence in another Contracting State*",[125] a status prescribed by the Practical Handbook an unaccompanied minor. This provision ensures that information-sharing mechanisms are in place to prevent further harm and facilitate appropriate protective measures across borders. In example, under Article 6(1), if a child, arrives in a contracting State fleeing conflict and without guardianship, the authorities of that State have jurisdiction to appoint a guardian and take necessary protective measures. This facilitates access to essential legal and social services, such as applying for refugee status. Analogously, under Article 6(2), the authorities of the State where the child is present may take necessary protection measures, even if it is later determined that the child's habitual residence is in another country including a non-contracting State,[126] these measures remain in force unless overridden by a decision from that non-contracting State. As such, the recognition and enforcement of any such foreign decision will depend on the national laws of the contracting State where the child is present.

In summary, the 1996 Hague Child Convention plays a vital role in safeguarding unaccompanied minors in cross-border situations. By providing legal mechanisms for cooperation, addressing jurisdictional challenges, and ensuring information exchange, the Convention strengthens the international framework for child protection. Its

---

124 Article 36, 1996 Hague Convention.

125 Explanatory Report, para 150.

126 Ibid, referencing Working Document No.83 acceding to proposal by Burkina Faso delegate.

implementation is particularly crucial in regions experiencing significant child migration, reinforcing global efforts to protect vulnerable children and uphold their fundamental rights.

# CHAPTER ELEVEN

# GUIDANCE AND COLLABORATION

## 11.1 Directives from the President of the Family Division

### 11.1.1 Guidance on Public Law Children Cases with an International Element

The 2025 President's Guidance on public law cases with an international element[127] explores, amongst others, the practical application of the 1996 Hague Convention regarding international child protection. It outlines key procedural steps for UK courts, emphasizing the role of the International Child Abduction and Contact Unit (ICACU) in facilitating cooperation across borders. The guidance encourages effective communication between courts, streamlined case handling, and proper identification of jurisdictional issues, ensuring the protection of children's welfare in cross-border family disputes. It also details ICACU's responsibilities in managing international cases.

The Guidance highlights that requests for co-operation must be *"relevant, focussed, timely and practical"*[128] and signposts practitioners

---

127 Sir Andrew McFarlane, "*President's Guidance: Public law children cases with an international element*" (January 2025). Referred to as "2025 ICACU President Guidance". Available at <https://www.judiciary.uk/wp-content/uploads/2025/01/PFD-ICACU-Guidance.pdf> replacing the President's Guidance of 10 November 2014.

128 Ibid, pg. 4

to the appropriate request for cooperation forms published which is to be completed and emailed, for England[129] and for Wales.[130] A key observation that will serve practitioners well in timely applications is noting that the 1996 Hague Convention does not mandate a specific timeline for a requested State to respond to a request for cooperation. While the requesting central authority cannot compel a response by a certain date, a well-focused and timely request is more likely to elicit a positive and prompt response from the relevant foreign authorities.[131]

In a public law case, the process involves a local authority requesting cooperation, with the English/Welsh Central Authority facilitating translation and transmission to the requested Central Authority. The requested authority makes inquiries and sends a response, which may require further translation before being sent back to the local authority. Additional guidance on the exchange of information is set out in summary as follows[132]:

a) Avoid acronyms and technical terms, or explain them if used (e.g., "viability assessment").

b) For "connected persons assessments," clarify what the local authority or court needs but avoid asking foreign authorities to complete domestic forms.

---

129 https://www.gov.uk/government/publications/international-child-abduction-unit-request-for-co-operation-form

130 https://www.gov.wales/handling-cross-border-child-protection-cases

131 2025 ICACU President Guidance, pg.4.

132 2025 ICACU President Guidance, pg. 5.

c) Provide as much information as possible to help trace potential carers, including last known addresses or identity details.

d) If you've contacted the connected person, share details of the communication.

e) Obtain court permission for disclosing information to authorities promptly.

Regarding the placement of a child abroad under Article 33,[133] the guidance highlights the importance of reviewing this provision as the other country may require consent before finalizing the placement. Whether the placement is considered foster care or institutional care is determined by the requested country. The guide notes that a placement considered private law in the domestic context may be viewed as public law abroad. If the care plan is incomplete, a request for cooperation can clarify if consent is necessary. When requesting a 'connected persons assessment,' also inquire about the Article 33 consent process.

The Guidance also notes that ICACU[134] has no role to play in the operation of the 1970 Convention on the Taking of Evidence Abroad in Civil and Commercial Matters and will not assist in the acquiring of evidence. The Central Authority for England and Wales is appointed solely to handle cases under the 1980 Hague Child Abduction Convention and 1996 Hague Child Protection Convention. However, should circumstances arise where either of

---

133 Ibid, pg. 6–7.

134 The international Child Abduction and Contact Unit (ICACU) for England and Wales.

these treaties intersect with the 1970 Convention,[135] a question that bears considering is what forum should take precedence especially when the interests of a child are at stake, and the case at risk of considerable delay.[136]

### 11.1.2 Guidance on the Transfer of Proceedings under Articles 8 and/or 9 of the 1996 Hague Convention

Guidance from the President of the Family Division[137] addresses the transfer of proceedings under Articles 8 and 9 of the 1996 Hague Convention. It provides procedural steps for both outgoing and incoming requests for the transfer of jurisdiction between England and Wales and other contracting States. The process includes notification, hearings, and coordination with Central Authorities like ICACU or the Welsh Government. The 2025 Transfer President Guidance emphasizes the importance of early preparation and clear communication when making or responding to jurisdictional transfer requests, and it outlines the role of the High Court in determining

---

135 See Momoh.O, *When two worlds collide: the 1970 Hague Evidence Convention and the 1980 Hague Child Abduction Convention*, [2025] Family Law Journal (Lexis Nexis).

136 2025 ICACU President Guidance, pg.3. Note that ICACU as designated in 1980 and 1996 Hague children cases is distinguishable from the appointed 'Central Authority' in 1970 Hague Evidence Convention cases. For England and Wales, it is the Senior Master at the Foreign Process Section (RCJ) <https://www.hcch.net/en/States/authorities/details3/?aid=526>

137 Sir Andrew McFarlane, "*Guidance from the President of the Family Division: Transfer of proceedings*", (January 2025). Referred to as "2025 Transfer President Guidance" Available at <https://www.judiciary.uk/guidance-and-resources/guidance-from-the-president-of-the-family-division-transfer-of-proceedings/>

incoming requests, as well as the appropriate process in outgoing requests.

## 11.2 International Social Services – CFAB

Children and Families Across Borders ("CFAB"), the UK branch of the International Social Service global network, is a non-governmental organisation which seeks to protects the rights of families affected by international separation. It provides inter-country casework, training, and advice to authorities, legal professionals, and families. CFAB also offers a free helpline for those facing cross-border family issues. Practitioners may be assisted by referring to publications such as CFAB's International Kinship Care Guide, "*A Good Practice Guide for Professionals Placing Children from Local Authority Care with Family Members Abroad,*" November 2020,[138] and CFAB's report entitled *"Cross-border Child Safeguarding: Challenges, Effective Social Work Practice and Outcomes for Children*" (2018).[139] The report sets out the findings of a study conducted on cross-border children and family cases. The report concludes with recommendations on addressing challenges and engaging in good practice amongst local authorities in managing such cases. At paragraph 7.4, it is stated that:

> *UK local authorities had different approaches to completing kinship assessments abroad, noticeably in the use of UK or overseas social workers and the level of assessment that was acceptable. The types of court order used for children placed abroad also varied (notably Child Arrangements Order vs Special*

---

138 Available at <https://www.cfab.org.uk/resources/international-kinship-care-guide>

139 Available at <https://assets.website-files.com/5f35add6489ebf598108eb78/60f4e08763657bb4c2811ef8_Cross%20Border%20Child%20Safeguarding%20-%20Research.pdf>

*Guardianship Order), as did levels of post-placement support provided, with some local authorities offering no post-placement support. It was notable that many local authorities who use overseas social workers to complete the assessment are supplementing this by inviting the prospective family member to travel to the UK for further assessment with the local authority social worker. This practice was also identified as good practice by professionals in the focus groups as it enabled time for introductions between the child and prospective carer before the placement.*

*Recommendation 4: The impact of the different approaches to assessments on the viability of prospective carers should be explored, in particular how the use of UK social workers to assess family members who reside abroad (whether the assessment is completed overseas or in the UK) affects the viability of the placement. CFAB recommends that this should be addressed in the DFE guidance "Working with foreign authorities: child protection cases and care orders."*

*In this case, it is likely that CAFCASS would be the relevant professional within private law proceedings, though it is not usual for welfare reports (under section 7 of the Children Act 1989) to be completed by local authorities. Situations such as these usually occur because of i.e., a previous involvement in the child or family's life.*[140]

*Recommendation 5: In addition, clearer guidance is needed into appropriate legal orders for international placements and how local authorities can continue to offer post-placement support even*

140 Family Court Bench Book, Judicial College, January 2018, page 80 https://www.judiciary.uk/wp-content/uploads/2016/10/family-court-bench-book-jan-2018.pdf

*when a child is placed abroad. CFAB recommends that this should be addressed in the DFE guidance "Working with foreign authorities: child protection cases and care orders.*

Furthermore, good practice[141] in international placement suggests that authorities should agree on a specific timeframe for UK Local Authorities to retain responsibility. A key example of ongoing responsibility is financial support under a Special Guardianship package approved during proceedings:

> "*It is recommended that the involvement of a local authority permanency team, or associated financial support, is longer than what would be expected in domestic placements particularly as domestic placements are likely to have been previously tested – which is not possible in international placements. In England, Special Guardianship support is the responsibility of the placing authority for three years. Given the additional risks associated with an overseas placement, the local authority may be involved for a longer period of time as it is their duty of care to the child to ensure they are in a good placement.*"

## 11.3 Central Authority

Under the 1996 Hague Convention, contracting States must designate a Central Authority to discharge the duties imposed by the Convention.[142] The International Child Abduction and Contact Unit ("ICACU") serves as the Central Authority for England, facilitating essential cooperation between jurisdictions. For Wales it is the Social

---

141 Pg.18 <https://assets.website-files.com/5f35add5341cd54e7d5d2386/60f4cd7b66b9ba45ad5f6c56_IKC%20Guide%20Nov%202020.pdf#page22>

142 Article 29(1), 1996 Hague Convention.

Serviced and Integration department within the Welsh Government.[143] In States with multiple legal systems, such as federal States or those with autonomous territorial units, more than one Central Authority may be designated. These authorities must cooperate and designate a primary authority to manage communications across their respective jurisdictions. Articles 29 to 39 of the 1996 Hague Convention outline the framework for cooperation between authorities. For example, in discharging its duties under the Convention (see Chapter V of the 1996 Hague Convention), ICACU facilitates the effective exchange of information, as well as assisting with the process of applying for the declared enforceability or registration of orders. Recent 2025 publications from the President, Sir Andrew McFarlane, "*President's Guidance: Public law children cases with an international element*" and "*Guidance from the President of the Family Division: Transfer of proceedings*" amply sets out tailored guidance on the operation of ICACU and other competent authorities such as the judiciary. Contact details for all designated Central Authorities can be found on the HCCH's specialised page for the 1996 Hague Convention. For England and for Wales these are a s follows:[144]

143 See HCCH "United Kingdom – Central Authority (Art. 29)", which also includes Central Authorities for Northern Ireland, Gibraltar and Scotland. <https://www.hcch.net/en/States/authorities/details3/?aid=941> last updated 03.07.2023.

144 As well as the 1980 Hague Convention.

England

Office of the Official Solicitor & Public Trustee
Post Point 0.53
102 Petty France
London
SW1H 9AJ
DX: Post Point 0.53 Official Solicitor & Public Trustee DX 152380
Westminster 8
United Kingdom
Tel: +44 (203) 681 2756
Email: icacu@ospt.gov.uk

Wales

Welsh Government Social Services and Integration
Cathays Park
Cardiff CF10 3NQ
United Kingdom
Tel: +44 3000 257095
Email: WalesCAHague1996@gov.wales

## 11.4 Department of Education

It is important to highlight key guidance issued by the Department for Education following the UK's implementation of the 1996 Hague Convention. Despite significant legal and procedural changes, including the UK's exit from the EU, these documents remain valuable resources, especially for administrative processes. Over time, the Department for Education has published various materials, including two key documents that continue to be accessible on their website. The *Department for Education guidance on Cross-border child protection cases: the 1996 Hague Convention* (October 2012)[145] was designed to support local authorities, social workers, service managers, and children's services lawyers by outlining how the Convention operates in managing international child protection matters. Additionally, the *Department for Education guidance on Working with foreign authorities: child protection cases and care orders* (July 2014)[146] provides further guidance for professionals navigating cross-border child protection cases. While these documents should be read in conjunction with subsequent legal developments and reviews, they provide a foundational understanding of key procedures. Local authorities must, of course, seek legal advice in individual cases where necessary. Nonetheless, these resources offer practical starting points for managing cross-border child protection cases, providing roadmaps and covering topics such as international cooperation, procedural responsibilities, and even guidance on subcontracting local authority work to external agencies.

---

146 <https://assets.publishing.service.gov.uk/media/5a7bff1be5274a7318b90648/The_1996_Hague_Convention.pdf> set for review in April 2014

146 <https://assets.publishing.service.gov.uk/media/5a7d9d2fe5274a676d5331a3/Working_with_Foreign_Authorities_-_Child_Protection_and_Court_Orders.pdf> set for review in July 2015

# CHAPTER TWELVE

# CONCLUSION

The 1996 Hague Convention addresses the increasing complexities of international child protection cases. As cross-border cases involving children continue to rise – added to the changing landscape following the UK's withdrawal from the EU – reliance on the Convention has become even more pronounced. It provides a comprehensive legal framework to safeguard children's rights and welfare across jurisdictions, ensuring that protective measures taken in one country are recognized and upheld in another. In England and Wales, the 1996 Hague Convention is an essential tool in public law proceedings, particularly where cross-border elements complicate decision-making. A wealth of resources have since emerged, *inter-alia*, case law developments that have offered valuable roadmaps for practitioners seeking to secure the best possible outcomes for children. The Convention establishes jurisdictional rules and promotes international cooperation, thereby reducing legal uncertainty and ensuring timely interventions in the child's best interest. One of its key strengths lies in clarifying which country has jurisdiction over a child's welfare when multiple legal systems are engaged. The Convention is also especially relevant in cases involving potential international kinship placements, covering collaborative welfare assessments, as well as enforcement of public law orders (or private orders made within care proceedings). The Convention ensures that placements overseas are conducted lawfully, coordinating between authorities and seeking consent where necessary.

Despite its strengths, it is not without its challenges. Differences in national legal systems, procedural delays, and variations in the interpretation of child welfare principles can hinder effective cooperation. Moreover, not all countries have ratified or acceded to the Convention, requiring reliance on diplomatic channels or bilateral agreements in certain cases. Indeed, encouraging international participation remains a key priority for the HCCH. Nevertheless, from an English perspective, the principles and mechanisms established by the Convention are indispensable in securing the safety, stability, and well-being of children in transnational situations.

# MORE BOOKS BY LAW BRIEF PUBLISHING

A selection of our other titles available now:-

| |
|---|
| 'A Practical Guide to Probation Breaches and Other Applications' by Mark Thomas |
| 'A Practical Guide to Remarriage and Divorce' by Cordelia Williams & Claire Howard |
| 'A Practical Guide to Privacy, Transparency, Reporting Restrictions and Closed Proceedings in the Court of Protection' by Laura Mannering |
| 'Beaumont on Barristers – A Guide to Defending Disciplinary Proceedings (Second Edition)' by Marc Beaumont |
| 'A Practical Guide to Payments for Environmental Services' by Ben Sharples |
| 'A Practical Guide to the Law of Pregnancy and Maternity at Work' by Rebecca Thomas |
| 'A Practical Guide to Redundancy – Second Edition' by Philip Hyland & Collette Moore |
| 'A Practical Guide to International Issues for Scottish Family Lawyers' by Susie Mountain, Donna McKay, Ken MacDonald |
| 'A Practical Guide to the Law on Deprivation of Liberty' by Ben Troke |
| 'A Practical Guide to Rights over Airspace and Subsoil – Second Edition' by Daniel Gatty |
| 'A Practical Guide to the Law in Relation to Inquests' by Ramya Nagesh |
| 'A Practical Guide to the Construction and Rectification of Wills and Trust Instruments (Second Edition)' by Edward Hewitt |
| 'A Practical Guide to Data Protection in Social Housing' by Clare Paterson |
| 'A Practical Guide to Spousal Maintenance – Second Edition' by Liz Cowell |
| 'A Practical Guide to International Parental Child Abduction Law (England and Wales)' by Dr Onyója Momoh |
| 'A Practical Guide to Deprivation of British Citizenship' by Sean Ell |
| 'A Practical Guide to Commercial Property Service Charges' by Rachel Garton |
| 'A Practical Guide to Clinical Negligence – Third Edition' by Geoffrey Simpson-Scott (Geoff) |
| 'A Practical Guide to the Rights of Grandparents in Children Proceedings – Second Edition' by Stuart Barlow |

| |
|---|
| 'The Electronic Communications Code: A Practical Guide – Second Edition' by Kerry Bretherton KC, James Castle, Mark Loveday |
| 'A Practical Guide to the Independent School Standards – September 2023 Edition' by Sarah McKimm |
| 'A Practical Guide to Estate Administration and Crypto Assets' by Richard Marshall |
| 'A Practical Guide to Parental Alienation in Private and Public Law Children Cases' by Sam King QC & Frankie Shama |
| 'Contested Heritage – Removing Art from Land and Historic Buildings' by Richard Harwood QC, Catherine Dobson, David Sawtell |
| 'The Limits of Separate Legal Personality: When Those Running a Company Can Be Held Personally Liable for Losses Caused to Third Parties Outside of the Company' by Dr Mike Wilkinson |
| 'A Practical Guide to Transgender Law' by Robin Moira White & Nicola Newbegin |
| 'A Practical Guide to 'Stranded Spouses' in Family Law' by Mani Singh Basi |
| 'A Practical Guide to Residential Freehold Conveyancing' by Lorraine Richardson |
| 'A Practical Guide to Pensions on Divorce for Lawyers' by Bryan Scant |
| 'A Practical Guide to Challenging Sham Marriage Allegations in Immigration Law' by Priya Solanki |
| 'A Practical Guide to Digital Communications Evidence in Criminal Law' by Sam Willis |
| 'A Practical Guide to Legal Rights in Scotland' by Sarah-Jane Macdonald |
| 'A Practical Guide to New Build Conveyancing' by Paul Sams & Rebecca East |
| 'A Practical Guide to Inherited Wealth on Divorce' by Hayley Trim |
| 'A Practical Guide to Practice Direction 12J and Domestic Abuse in Private Law Children Proceedings' by Rebecca Cross & Malvika Jaganmohan |
| 'A Practical Guide to Confiscation and Restraint' by Narita Bahra QC, John Carl Townsend, David Winch |
| 'A Practical Guide to the Law of Forests in Scotland' by Philip Buchan |
| 'A Practical Guide to Health and Medical Cases in Immigration Law' by Rebecca Chapman & Miranda Butler |
| 'A Practical Guide to Bad Character Evidence for Criminal Practitioners by Aparna Rao |
| 'A Practical Guide to Extradition Law post-Brexit' by Myles Grandison et al |
| 'A Practical Guide to Hoarding and Mental Health for Housing Lawyers' by Rachel Coyle |

| |
|---|
| 'Stephens on Contractual Indemnities' by Richard Stephens |
| 'A Practical Guide to the EU Succession Regulation' by Richard Frimston |
| 'A Practical Guide to Solicitor and Client Costs – Second Edition' by Robin Dunne |
| 'Constructive Dismissal – Practice Pointers and Principles' by Benjimin Burgher |
| 'A Practical Guide to Religion and Belief Discrimination Claims in the Workplace' by Kashif Ali |
| 'A Practical Guide to the Law of Medical Treatment Decisions' by Ben Troke |
| 'Fundamental Dishonesty and QOCS in Personal Injury Proceedings: Law and Practice' by Jake Rowley |
| 'A Practical Guide to the Law in Relation to School Exclusions' by Charlotte Hadfield & Alice de Coverley |
| 'A Practical Guide to Divorce for the Silver Separators' by Karin Walker |
| 'The Right to be Forgotten – The Law and Practical Issues' by Melissa Stock |
| 'A Practical Guide to Planning Law and Rights of Way in National Parks, the Broads and AONBs' by James Maurici QC, James Neill et al |
| 'A Practical Guide to Election Law' by Tom Tabori |
| 'A Practical Guide to the Law in Relation to Surrogacy' by Andrew Powell |
| 'A Practical Guide to Claims Arising from Fatal Accidents – Second Edition' by James Patience |
| 'A Practical Guide to Asbestos Claims' by Jonathan Owen & Gareth McAloon |
| 'A Practical Guide to Stamp Duty Land Tax in England and Northern Ireland' by Suzanne O'Hara |
| 'A Practical Guide to the Law of Farming Partnerships' by Philip Whitcomb |
| 'A Practical Guide to the Law of Unlawful Eviction and Harassment – Second Edition' by Stephanie Lovegrove |
| 'A Practical Guide to Costs in Personal Injury Claims – Second Edition' by Matthew Hoe |
| 'A Practical Guide to the General Data Protection Regulation (GDPR) – Second Edition' by Keith Markham |
| 'A Practical Guide to Working with Litigants in Person and McKenzie Friends in Family Cases' by Stuart Barlow |
| 'Protecting Unregistered Brands: A Practical Guide to the Law of Passing Off' by Lorna Brazell |
| 'A Practical Guide to Secondary Liability and Joint Enterprise Post-Jogee' by Joanne Cecil & James Mehigan |

'A Practical Guide to the Pre-Action RTA Claims Protocol for Personal Injury Lawyers' by Antonia Ford

'A Practical Guide to Neighbour Disputes and the Law' by Alexander Walsh

'A Practical Guide to Coercive Control for Legal Practitioners and Victims' by Rachel Horman

'A Practical Guide to the Law of Driverless Cars – Second Edition'

by Alex Glassbrook, Emma Northey & Scarlett Milligan

'A Practical Guide to TOLATA Claims' by Greg Williams

'A Practical Guide to Elderly Law – Second Edition' by Justin Patten

'A Practical Guide to Responding to Housing Disrepair and Unfitness Claims' by Iain Wightwick

'A Practical Guide to the Law of Bullying and Harassment in the Workplace' by Philip Hyland

'How to Be a Freelance Solicitor: A Practical Guide to the SRA-Regulated Freelance Solicitor Model' by Paul Bennett

'A Practical Guide to Prison Injury Claims' by Malcolm Johnson

'A Practical Guide to Advising Clients at the Police Station' by Colin Stephen McKeown-Beaumont

'A Practical Guide to Antisocial Behaviour Injunctions – Second Edition' by Iain Wightwick

'Practical Mediation: A Guide for Mediators, Advocates, Advisers, Lawyers, and Students in Civil, Commercial, Business, Property, Workplace, and Employment Cases' by Jonathan Dingle with John Sephton

'The Mini-Pupillage Workbook' by David Boyle

'A Practical Guide to Crofting Law' by Brian Inkster

'A Practical Guide to the Law of Domain Names and Cybersquatting' by Andrew Clemson

'A Practical Guide to the Law of Gender Pay Gap Reporting' by Harini Iyengar

'NHS Whistleblowing and the Law' by Joseph England

'Employment Law and the Gig Economy' by Nigel Mackay & Annie Powell

'A Practical Guide to Noise Induced Hearing Loss (NIHL) Claims' by Andrew Mckie, Ian Skeate, Gareth McAloon

'An Introduction to Beauty Negligence Claims – A Practical Guide for the Personal Injury Practitioner' by Greg Almond

'Intercompany Agreements for Transfer Pricing Compliance' by Paul Sutton

'Zen and the Art of Mediation' by Martin Plowman

'A Practical Guide to Adoption for Family Lawyers' by Graham Pegg

| |
|---|
| 'A Practical Guide to Industrial Disease Claims' by Andrew Mckie & Ian Skeate |
| 'A Practical Guide to Conducting a Sheriff Court Proof' by Andrew Stevenson |
| 'A Practical Guide to Vicarious Liability' by Mariel Irvine |
| 'A Practical Guide to Applications for Landlord's Consent and Variation of Leases' by Mark Shelton |
| 'A Practical Guide to Relief from Sanctions Post-Mitchell and Denton' by Peter Causton |
| 'A Practical Guide to Equity Release for Advisors' by Paul Sams |
| 'A Practical Guide to Financial Services Claims' by Chris Hegarty |
| 'A Practical Guide to Financial Ombudsman Service Claims' by Adam Temple & Robert Scrivenor |
| 'A Practical Guide to Running Housing Disrepair and Cavity Wall Claims – Second Edition' by Andrew Mckie & Ian Skeate |
| 'A Practical Guide to Holiday Sickness Claims – Second Edition' by Andrew Mckie & Ian Skeate |
| 'Arguments and Tactics for Personal Injury and Clinical Negligence Claims' by Dorian Williams |
| 'A Practical Guide to Drone Law' by Rufus Ballaster, Andrew Firman, Eleanor Clot |
| 'On Experts: CPR35 for Lawyers and Experts' by David Boyle |
| 'An Introduction to Personal Injury Law' by David Boyle |

These books and more are available to order online direct from the publisher at www.lawbriefpublishing.com, where you can also read free sample chapters. For any queries, call us on 0844 587 2383 or email us at mail@lawbriefpublishing.com.

Our books are all generally in stock at www.amazon.co.uk with free next day delivery for Prime members, and at good legal bookshops such as Wildy & Sons.

We are regularly launching new books in our series of practical day-to-day practitioners' guides. Visit our website and join our free newsletter to be kept informed and to receive special offers, free chapters, etc.

You can also follow us on Twitter at www.twitter.com/lawbriefpub.

www.ingramcontent.com/pod-product-compliance
Lightning Source LLC
LaVergne TN
LVHW022109200926
848481LV00003B/1127